F

ONE WEEK LOAN

Other titles available from Law Society Publishing:

Civil Partnership
Andrea Woelke

Domestic Abuse
Jane Wilson

Good Practice in Child Care Cases (2nd edn)
The Law Society

Pensions and Family Breakdown (2nd edn)
David Davidson

Resolution Family Disputes Handbook
General Editor: Andrew Greensmith

Resolution Family Law Handbook (2nd edn)
General Editor: Andrew Greensmith

Tax and Family Breakdown
Jason Lane

Titles from Law Society Publishing can be ordered from all good bookshops or direct (telephone 0870 850 1422, email **lawsociety@prolog.uk.com** or visit our online shop at **www.lawsociety.org.uk/bookshop**).

FAMILY LAW PROTOCOL

THIRD EDITION

The Law Society

The Law Society

© The Law Society 2010

Crown copyright material is reproduced with the permission of the Controller of Her Majesty's Stationery Office

ISBN-13: 978-1-85328-884-5

Published in 2010 by the Law Society
113 Chancery Lane, London WC2A 1PL

Typeset by Columns Design XML Ltd, Reading
Printed by TJ International Ltd, Padstow, Cornwall

The paper used for the text pages of this book is FSC certified. FSC (the Forest Stewardship Council) is an international network to promote responsible management of the world's forests.

Contents

Foreword to the third edition by the Right Honourable Sir Nicholas Wall

It is five years since the second edition of the Law Society's Family Law Protocol and much has changed in the law and practice of family law. However, some aspects remain unaltered and in the second edition, Sir Mark Potter stated: 'I commend the Protocol's emphasis on attempting to achieve resolution by means of ADR and its insistence that court proceedings should be a last resort.' Five years on, I repeat and fully endorse this requirement upon solicitors.

The Protocol distils the important elements of practice and procedure, and provides clear and helpful guidance to family practitioners. Adherence to **Part 1** will assist them in achieving the 'overriding objective' to enable courts to deal with cases justly.

I recommend this good practice guide to all who work within the field of family law.

Nicholas Wall
President of the Family Division
November 2010

Preface and acknowledgements

The publication of the first edition of the Family Law Protocol in 2002 broke new ground. It was a bold attempt to provide an overall view of good practice in family law matters. Although specifically referring to solicitors, it was designed to offer guidance to all family practitioners working in solicitors' firms, whether legal executives, paralegals or clerks. It was pleasing to find that its publication was almost universally applauded. The number of endorsements received for it was impressive, and the lectures around the country that accompanied its launch were well received.

The Law Society updated the Protocol in 2005 and since then a significant number of changes have taken place and a number of changes are still pending. It is also fair to note that despite the comprehensive nature of the previous two editions of the Protocol, it quickly became apparent that there are many areas of family law that were still not covered.

The redrafting of the Protocol has enabled many amendments to be made. Some are amendments arising out of experience. Others come from significant changes to the law that have been enacted, such as:

- the introduction of the Public Law Outline and its impact on care proceedings;
- changes affecting pre-nuptial agreements and pension orders;
- the introduction of civil partnerships and their dissolution;
- permitted attendance of media representatives at hearings in family proceedings; and
- the introduction of applications for forced marriage protection orders.

In addition, the third edition has been expanded to include new chapters on:

- child support;
- Children Act 1989, Schedule 1 proceedings; and
- family agreements

The main protocol in **Part 1** has been significantly amended, shortened and is endorsed by the President of the Family Division. The Protocol is the standard by which members of the Law Society and Resolution are judged, and therefore is the standard to which legal aid practitioners are expected to practise. There may be reasons to depart from the Protocol, but the onus is on those wishing to depart to justify their position.

The third edition of the Family Law Protocol has been produced by the Law Society, with the close involvement of Resolution. The aims and scope of this Protocol remain as they did for the first edition.

Acknowledgements

The Law Society's Family Law Protocol was drafted by the following the Law Society Family Law Committee:

- Naomi Angell
- Nicholas Aspley
- Christina Blacklaws
- James Carroll
- Graham Cole
- Stuart Collingham
- Barbara Corbett
- Judith Crisp
- Robin ap Cynan
- Godfrey Freeman
- Emma Hitchings
- Robert Hush
- Sunita Mason
- David Woodward

with the assistance of the following Resolution members:

- Helen Blackburn
- Punam Denley
- Angela Donen
- Oliver Gravell
- Emma Harte
- Steve Kirwan
- Vicki McLynn
- James Pirrie
- Hannah Perry
- Neil Robinson
- Nigel Shepherd
- Jane Wilson.

The Committee would like to thank Jacqui Jackson for co-ordinating the invaluable input of her Resolution colleagues as well as Andrew Greensmith, partner at Dickson Haslam and chair of the publications committee at Resolution for his assistance in general editing this edition of the Family Law Protocol.

The Protocol is endorsed by:

- The Rt Hon Sir Nicholas Wall, President of the Family Division
- The Rt Hon Lord Justice Matthew Thorpe, Deputy Head of Family Justice and Head of International Family Law
- Association of Lawyers for Children
- Children and Family Court Advisory and Support Service (Cafcass)
- Family Law Bar Association
- Official Solicitor
- Resolution.

November 2010

Table of cases

Table of statutes

Table of statutory instruments

Table of international instruments

Abbreviations

ACA 2002	Adoption and Children Act 2002
ACTAPS	Association of Contentious Trust and Probate Specialists
ADR	alternative dispute resolution
Cafcass	Children and Family Court Advisory and Support Service
CAO	child assessment order
CFL	collaborative family law
CMEC	Child Maintenance and Enforcement Commission
CPR	Civil Procedure Rules 1998
CMOPA 2008	Child Maintenance and Other Payments Act 2008
CPS	Crown Prosecution Service
CSA	Child Support Agency
CSAT	Child Support Appeal Tribunal
EPO	emergency protection order
FDA	first directions appointment
FDR	financial dispute resolution
FHDRA	first hearing dispute resolution appointment
FLA 1986	Family Law Act 1986
FLA 1996	Family Law Act 1996
FMA	Family Mediators Association
FMC	Family Mediation Council
FP(A)R 2005	Family Procedure (Adoption) Rules 2005
FPCR 1991	Family Proceedings Courts (Children Act 1989) Rules 1991
FPR 1991	Family Proceedings Rules 1991
HFEA 2008	Human Fertilisation and Embryology Act 2008
ICACU	International Child Abduction and Contact Unit
IHT	inheritance tax
I(PFD)A 1975	Inheritance (Provision for Family and Dependants) Act 1975
LR(MP)A 1970	Law Reform (Miscellaneous Provisions) Act 1970
LSC	Legal Services Commission
MCA 1973	Matrimonial Causes Act 1973
MPPA 1970	Matrimonial Proceedings and Property Act 1970
MWPA 1882	Married Women's Property Act 1882
NACCC	National Association of Child Contact Centres

NACSA	National Association for Child Support Action
NFM	National Family Mediation
NRP	non-resident parent
NSPCC	National Society for the Prevention of Cruelty to Children
PIP	Parenting Information Programme
PWC	parent with care
SGO	special guardianship orders
TLATA 1996	Trusts of Land and Appointment of Trustees Act 1996

PART 1

Main protocol

1.1 SCOPE

1.1.1 This chapter details those overarching matters family lawyers must consider in order to promote their clients' best interests. The subsequent chapters provide a wealth of information as regards particular areas of practice.

1.2 RESOLUTION CODE OF PRACTICE

1.2.1 The Family Law Protocol endorses the Resolution Code of Practice, namely a commitment to resolve a dispute in a non-confrontational and constructive way to preserve people's dignity and to encourage agreements.

The Resolution Code of Practice is set out in full at **www.resolution.org.uk**.

1.3 GUIDES TO GOOD PRACTICE

1.3.1 The following books have been published by the Law Society:

- *Good Practice in Child Care Cases* (2nd edn, Law Society, 2010).
- *Resolution Family Law Handbook* (2nd edn, Law Society, 2010).
- *Resolution Family Disputes Handbook* (2nd edn, Law Society, 2010).

1.3.2 The following Resolution guides are to be found on the public part of the Resolution website at **www.resolution.org.uk**:

- Dealing with Clients
- Correspondence
- Litigants in Person
- Working with the Bar

- Disclosure in Ancillary Relief
- Service in the Family Law Context

1.4 SOLICITORS REGULATION AUTHORITY

1.4.1 All solicitors must comply with:

- the Solicitors' Code of Conduct 2007 (at **www.sra.org.uk**); and
- the need to check for evidence of identity and address under the Money Laundering Regulations 2007, SI 2007/2157.

1.5 FIRST MEETING

Children

1.5.1 Do:

- emphasise the need for parents to accept parental responsibility for their children;
- promote the child's welfare as the paramount consideration;
- encourage separation of addressing the children's needs from those of the parents;
- encourage the use of mediation and other methods of dispute resolution;
- provide information about local support/guidance services;
- provide information about parenting apart.

Resolution has a dedicated information section on its website: **www.resolution.org.uk**.

Reconciliation

1.5.2 Do consider with the client whether their relationship is at an end and have available details of referral agencies who can assist.

Dispute resolution

1.5.3 Do consider with the client the following alternatives:

- agreement between the parties;
- negotiation between the parties' solicitors;
- mediation;
- collaborative law;

- family arbitration (when available);
- court application.

Inform the client that these may be used in combination and are not mutually exclusive.

Domestic abuse

1.5.4   Do be aware of:

- the incidents of domestic abuse, the need to screen for it and to make a risk assessment;
- the civil and criminal remedies.

Jurisdictional issues

1.5.5   Do consider if there are such issues including, for Europe, the impact of EU Council Regulation (EC) 2201/2003 ('Brussels II revised').

1.6   CLIENTS UNDER A LEGAL DISABILITY

1.6.1   Solicitors must bear in mind that they cannot be retained by clients incapable of giving instructions (Solicitors' Code of Conduct 2007, rule 2.01(6)(a)(iii) and rule 2.01(10)). Such clients will be those under 18 (subject to the provisions of the Family Proceedings Rules (FPR) 1991, SI 1991/1247, rule 9.2A and the Family Procedure (Adoption) Rules (FP(A)R) 2005, SI 2005/2795, rule 51) and may be those with learning disability, mental health problems, brain injury (including dementia) or any combination of these difficulties, if they come within the definition of 'protected party' as set out in FPR 1991, rule 9.1 and FP(A)R 2005, rule 6. A solicitor consulted by a client who cannot give instructions must identify a willing and suitable next friend/guardian ad litem/litigation friend (hereafter all referred to as 'litigation friend') to conduct any litigation (FPR 1991, rule 9.2; FP(A)R 2005, rule 50). The Official Solicitor is the litigation friend of last resort. He will act in the absence of anyone else willing and suitable (see *Practice Note (Official Solicitor: Appointment in Family Proceedings)* [2001] 2 FLR 155).

1.6.2   Equally, solicitors must be alert to any information suggesting that the other party may be under a disability and in need of a litigation friend. There are specific rules about the service of a petition on a person under a disability (FPR 1991, rule 9.3; see also FP(A)R 2005, rule 52(2)–(3) with regard to proceedings under the Adoption and Children Act 2002).

1.6.3 If a solicitor is in any doubt about whether a client (or the other party) is a protected party for the purposes of FPR 1991, rule 9.1 or FP(A)R 2005, rule 6, the Official Solicitor can provide his standard certificate of capacity to conduct the proceedings (and notes for guidance) to be completed by either an independent expert or a treating clinician.

1.6.4 Solicitors are reminded that when asking for an expert opinion on a party's capacity to conduct litigation it is the solicitor's responsibility to ensure that the expert is given the appropriate guidance as to the legal test. As part of that guidance the expert's attention should be drawn to the fact that the test for capacity is issue-specific. The expert should be provided with a description of the litigation in respect of which they are being asked to assess the client's litigation capacity, including a description of the issues which the client will be expected to understand and the decisions that will be required. Solicitors may find it helpful to refer to the May 2010 guidance published by the Public Law Committee of the Family Justice Council 'Parents who lack capacity to conduct public law proceedings' which annexes precedent letters of instruction and provides guidance on information to be given to the client about any assessment (available at **www.family-justice-council.org.uk/publications.htm**).

1.6.5 An application to the court for the appointment of a litigation friend pursuant to FPR 1991, rule 9.2 or FP(A)R 2005, rule 54 should be made at the earliest possible opportunity upon receipt of evidence confirming the client's incapacity.

1.6.6 In the event that such evidence is inconclusive or the solicitor has difficulties in obtaining such evidence, then the matter ought to be referred to the court for directions.

1.6.7 Solicitors may also find it helpful to refer to the website of the Official Solicitor (**www.officialsolicitor.gov.uk**); alternatively his office can be contacted for further guidance (see **Appendix B**).

1.6.8 Solicitors should bear in mind that they may be personally liable for costs for purporting to act without authority on behalf of a person under a disability, whether or not that disability has been established by medical evidence (*Yonge* v. *Toynbee* [1910] 1 KB 215).

1.7 CLIENT CARE

1.7.1 Rule 2.02 of the Solicitors' Code of Conduct 2007 states:

(1) You must:

      (a)   identify clearly the client's objectives in relation to the work to be done for the client;

      (b)   give the client a clear explanation of the issues involved and the options available to the client;

      (c)   agree with the client the next steps to be taken; and

      (d)   keep the client informed of progress, unless otherwise agreed.

(2)   You must, both at the outset and, as necessary, during the course of the matter:

      (a)   agree an appropriate level of service;

      (b)   explain your responsibilities;

      (c)   explain the client's responsibilities;

      (d)   ensure that the client is given, in writing, the name and status of the person dealing with the matter and the name of the person responsible for its overall supervision; and

      (e)   explain any limitations or conditions resulting from your relationship with a third party (for example a funder, fee sharer or introducer) which affect the steps you can take on the client's behalf.

1.8   COSTS

1.8.1   Rule 2.03 of the Solicitors' Code of Conduct 2007 states:

(1)   You must give your client the best information possible about the likely overall cost of the matter both at the outset and, when appropriate, as the matter progresses. In particular you must:

      (a)   advise the client of the basis and terms of your charges;

      (b)   advise the client if charging rates are to be increased:

      (c)   advise the client of likely payments which you or your client may need to make to others;

      (d)   discuss with the client how the client will pay, in particular:

          (i)   whether the client may be eligible and should apply for public funding; and

          (ii)   whether the client's own costs are covered by insurance or may be paid by someone else such as an employer or trade union;

      (e)   advise the client that there are circumstances where you may be entitled to exercise a lien for unpaid costs;

      (f)   advise the client of their potential liability for any other party's costs; and

      (g)   discuss with the client whether their liability for another party's costs may be covered by existing insurance or whether specially purchased insurance may be obtained.

Note the requirement at (1)(d)(i) to discuss eligibility for public funding and that this duty continues as the matter progresses.

1.8.2   It is essential to provide the client with a retainer letter setting out your standard terms of business and to comply with the above rule 2.02 and rule 2.03 requirements.

1.9   COMMUNICATION WITH THE OTHER PARTY AND LEGAL ADVISERS

1.9.1   Do:

- communicate in a non-confrontational and constructive manner designed to preserve dignity and encourage agreements;
- adopt the Resolution guide to good practice on correspondence at **www.resolution.org.uk**.

1.10   DEALING WITH LITIGANTS IN PERSON

1.10.1   There are an increasing number of litigants in person and 'McKenzie Friends' so the likelihood of finding yourself dealing with them is also increasing.

1.10.2   Successfully managing this challenge will help your client to achieve his/her objectives and setting the right tone at the outset is essential.

1.10.3   Patience, courtesy, good humour and an effort to understand why the person is not instructing a lawyer will get you off on 'the right foot'.

1.10.4   Do read the Resolution guide to good practice on dealing with litigants in person at **www.resolution.org.uk**.

1.10.5   Consider the President of the Family Division's *Guidance on McKenzie Friends* issued on 12 July 2010 (see **Appendix A**).

1.11   GIVING NOTICE OF THE ISSUE OF PROCEEDINGS

1.11.1   Prior to the issue of proceedings of any nature solicitors acting for applicants or petitioners should notify those acting for respondents (or respondents themselves where unrepresented) of the intention to commence proceedings at least seven days in advance unless there is good reason not to do so.

1.11.2   It is bad practice for proposed respondents to then issue proceedings to pre-empt the proposed application and this will result in:

- the court's disapproval;

- costs implications;
- greater difficulty in reaching agreement.

1.11.3 There may be good reason for breaching the above, particularly if Brussels II revised applies, but the onus is on the party in breach to justify their actions.

1.11.4 Do read Resolution guide to good practice on service at **www. resolution.org.uk**.

PART 2

Alternative dispute resolution

2.1 WHAT IS ALTERNATIVE DISPUTE RESOLUTION?

2.1.1 Alternative dispute resolution (ADR) comprises a range of options for resolving disputes without going to court. It ranges from direct negotiation between the parties via dispute resolution through mediation, collaborative law, early neutral evaluation, to arbitration and adjudication, all taking their places on an ADR continuum.

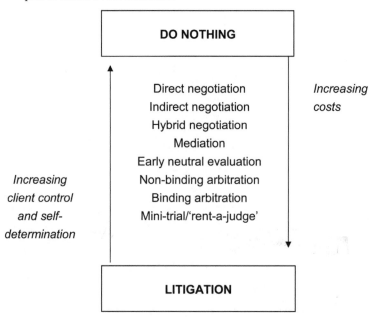

Note other hybrid processes (e.g. med-arb, family group conferencing)

Figure 2.1 ADR continuum

2.1.2 Within the field of family disputes the most common forms of family ADR are family mediation and collaborative family law (CFL). However, arbitration is also an option.

2.1.3 In arbitration an independent third party considers both sides in a dispute, and makes a decision that resolves the dispute. The arbitrator is impartial and does not take sides. There have been schemes for non-binding arbitration in family matters for many years, and a new scheme in which Resolution is involved is expected to start during the currency of this Protocol.

2.1.4 There are also those who consider that inter-solicitor negotiation may stand as an example of ADR since it does not necessarily involve the litigation process, however, inter-solicitor negotiation is more generally regarded as part of the mainstream of family law, and not as an ADR process or technique.

2.1.5 There are also ADR approaches which are built into, or can be accessed from certain parts of, the court processes for resolving family disputes. However, such ADR techniques applied within the court process are outside the scope of this section of the Family Law Protocol, although routes at court into ADR processes independent from the court process will be touched upon.

2.1.6 For more information about forms of family ADR, reference may be made to the Law Society's *Resolution Family Disputes Handbook* (2010).

2.2 FAMILY MEDIATION

Outline of family mediation

2.2.1 Mediation is the most established ADR technique. Mediators work as neutral third parties, with no stake in the outcome of the mediation process. They act as facilitators to the negotiations between the parties, providing information to assist when and if appropriate.

2.2.2 Family mediation is described in the Law Society Code of Practice for Family Mediation (July 2009) as:

a process in which:

1.1 a couple or any other family members
1.2 whether or not they are legally represented
1.3 and at any time, whether or not there are or have been legal proceedings
1.4 agree to the appointment of a neutral third party (the mediator)
1.5 who is impartial
1.6 who has no authority to make any decisions with regard to their issues

1.7 which may relate to separation, divorce, [relationship breakdown, dissolution of civil partnership,] children's issues, property and financial questions or any other issues they may raise

1.8 but who helps them reach their own informed decisions

1.9 by negotiation

1.10 without adjudication.

'Without adjudication'

2.2.3 Family mediation is generally considered to have four main principles – the voluntariness and the confidentiality (subject to exceptions) of the process, the impartiality of the mediator, and that decision making lies with the participants. Whilst the chief benefits of mediation include its creativity and flexibility, if the ADR process, however developed, lies outside those principles, it cannot be mediation and there will be insurance, funding and regulatory consequences. For the remainder of this section, the term 'mediation' means family mediation.

2.2.4 Mediation often involves a single mediator, but from time to time it may also involve two mediators co-mediating together, which is further discussed later in this section. However, for the remainder of this section, the term mediator will be used to include the situation where two mediators are co-mediating, unless otherwise distinguished.

2.2.5 From time to time the dispute between a couple may involve a wider group of family members than just the couple. Family members may include new partners, step-parents, grandparents, aunts, uncles, children (and young people), siblings and even potential family members. Any of these people may participate in the mediation with the agreement of the couple and the mediator.

2.2.6 Mediation may also take place between family members who have not been a couple (whether married, in a civil partnership or in any other cohabiting relationship) and who may or may not have been living under the same roof. Examples of this include an application by grandparents for contact with a grandchild, or by an adult child for financial provision from a parent for university fees or expenses.

2.2.7 Mediators do not routinely see children in mediation, but where they do, they usually see them as an adjunct to the process by way of separate consultation, rather than as children participating directly in the mediation. A mediator must only see children when the mediator is specifically trained in the involvement of children and young people in the mediation process. Mediators, like any other professionals who see children, must meet requirements in respect of police checks, etc. The same confidentiality applies to child consultation as to the rest of the process and feedback is only given from the consultation with the consent of the children.

Screening for mediation

2.2.8   Whilst it is certainly the case that there is now a greater expectation on the part of judges and the courts that a greater proportion of cases should attempt mediation, it is still important that only those cases that are suitable are referred.

2.2.9   At an early stage solicitors must, unless it is clearly inappropriate to do so (see **2.2.11**), explain the mediation process and advise clients on the benefits (including the benefits as to costs and as to timescale) and/or limitations of mediation in their particular case, as well as their own role as solicitors in supporting the mediation process.

2.2.10   Mediation can resolve issues in dispute or narrow those issues, but it may not be appropriate in some circumstances, at least until other steps (for example applying for interim maintenance, a freezing order or obtaining domestic protection) have been put in hand. Mediation is likely to be inappropriate:

- where there are unresolved child protection issues or a risk of child abduction;
- where clients do not have the capacity to mediate or their mental competence is in question;
- before emergency procedures which need to be taken have been concluded;
- where a particular issue can only be adjudicated upon by the court, for example, in paternity cases; or
- in financial proceedings where either party is bankrupt.

2.2.11   Mediation may also not be appropriate in the following circumstances:

1.   **Where domestic abuse has occurred or is still occurring.** If clients still wish to mediate in such cases, the risks should be considered and discussed as should whether any steps or actions can be taken to make them feel safe in the mediation. All mediators are well trained in recognising and categorising domestic abuse. (The term domestic abuse is defined in **Part 4** and guidance is given on screening, safety planning, etc.) Mediators will often categorise a matter as unsuitable for mediation by reason of domestic abuse. It is important, however, also to recognise the potential benefits of a robustly boundaried model of mediation to preserve parental relationships and communication in such circumstances, but all should be aware not only of the

basic principles of mediation but of recent guidance and case law regarding protection of children even when 'safe' agreements are purported to have been reached.

2. **Where the imbalance between parties is or may be such that the mediator(s) cannot rebalance it.** Solicitors should be aware of the need to consider mediation in certain publicly funded cases, where the issue of imbalance will be addressed by the mediators when screening the case for mediation suitability.

3. **Where relationship counselling or marital therapy may be more appropriate prior to mediation.**

This is not an all-inclusive list but covers most situations which may be unsuitable for mediation.

Which mediator?

2.2.12   Solicitors who refer clients to mediation should provide details of mediators who have undertaken appropriate training and/or have obtained accreditation with an established organisation. These details should be kept up to date. Details of the Law Society Family Mediation Panel and how to access its members may be found on the Law Society's website. Other organisations which offer family mediation training and accreditation include Family Mediators Association (FMA), National Family Mediation (NFM), the College of Mediators, ADR Group, and Resolution, for which contact details are set out in **Appendix B**. All six organisations (including the Law Society) are member organisations of the Family Mediation Council (FMC).

2.2.13   Family Mediation Competence Assessment Schemes are run by the Law Society (its Family Mediation Panel) and by the FMC. Both are recognised by the Legal Services Commission (LSC), and represent a prerequisite for offering publicly funded family mediation services. Despite the diversity of pathways into the mediation profession, it is likely that there will soon be a common standard of accreditation recognised for privately and publicly funded cases alike.

2.2.14   Mediators come into mediation from a range of professional disciplines, principally from having a legal background or from the field of counselling, therapy, psychology or social work. Different mediators may specialise in different types of family mediation, in exactly the same way as different solicitors may specialise in different types of family law.

2.2.15   Solicitors should advise and assist clients in selecting the most suitable family mediator/s for the dispute in question, by reference to some or all of the following aspects:

- training;
- areas of expertise;
- discipline(s);
- appreciation of relevant issues of ethnicity and culture;
- charging rates;
- geographical suitability;
- any other relevant characteristics.

2.2.16   Solicitors must advise clients who are eligible for public funding:

- as to the availability of publicly funded mediation;
- as to the fact that no contractual or statutory charge applies to the costs of publicly funded mediation;
- as to the fact that there are no contributions payable;
- as to their entitlement to legal advice in connection with the mediation under Level 2 funding;
- that non-contributory Level 2 funding also includes implementing the outcome of mediation into a legally binding court order if required;
- that in many circumstances where Level 2 funding is so used it too will be exempt from the statutory charge.

Different mediation models

Co-mediation

2.2.17   Some mediators consider a case is appropriate for co-mediation by two mediators, usually one of each gender (although not always the case with same-sex couples or with intergenerational mediation), and often from differing disciplines. Different mediation providers offer varying costings models for co-mediation – some offer co-mediation at the same fee as solo mediation, others charge a small premium, and some a significant premium. Publicly funded clients will not be subject to any additional charge or contribution where the LSC funds co-mediation.

2.2.18   Working in co-mediation can sometimes be quicker than working with a sole mediator (even a sole solicitor mediator) although fixing appointments may be more difficult at times with two diaries to consult. However, the most significant reason for working in co-mediation is the enhanced capacity it offers to the mediation provider to deal with couples where there are higher than usual levels of conflict and/or complexity, and in particular where a more resilient mediation process will allow clients to be better assisted where they are closer to the boundaries of suitability for mediation.

2.2.19   Some circumstances where co-mediation may be particularly helpful include:

- parties in high conflict;
- background of domestic abuse (also see **2.2.11**);
- emotional, legal or financial complexity;
- foreign element;
- emotional neediness;
- multi-party mediations;
- significant issues of culture or ethnicity;
- clients with complex disabilities.

2.2.20   How and when co-mediation may be appropriate will be determined by the mediation provider (or individual mediator) prior to mediation commencing and certainly in dialogue with the parties, although the decision as to the mediation model offered will ultimately be for the mediator/s.

Anchor mediation

2.2.21   'Anchor mediation' is an additional mediation model offered by many mediation services where there is an explicit arrangement with the parties that the mediation may take place with one or two mediators as the circumstances of the mediation require, however, one mediator (the 'anchor mediator') will be present throughout the mediation process, a second mediator being drawn in from time to time as may be helpful. Anchor mediation may commence with one or two mediators, the second mediator may be brought into (or withdrawn from) subsequent sessions, and fees adjusted accordingly.

2.2.22   Similar considerations apply to the use of anchor mediation as apply to the use of co-mediation.

2.2.23   How and when a second mediator is used in anchor mediation will be a decision for the anchor mediator in dialogue with the parties.

Mediating with legal representative in the mediation room

2.2.24   Family mediation only occasionally involves parties' legal representatives being present and working (whether as mediation advocates or otherwise) within the mediation room – unlike civil/commercial mediation, where it is the norm. However, there are no issues of principle within family mediation which render the presence of legal representatives 'at the mediation table' inappropriate or unworkable.

2.2.25   Where family mediators do work with legal representatives present during some or all of the mediation, the precise role for the legal representatives is individually determined for the individual mediation. They may be there to

14

provide *sotto voce* advice; they may be there to undertake mediation advocacy; they may be there as pure observers, to then proffer advice in caucus away from the mediation room (and see **2.2.27**).

2.2.26   There are however a small number of discrete principles concerning the presence of legal representatives in the family mediation room:

- LSC funding is explicitly available (within the standard fees at Level 2, and possibly at Level 3) to remunerate legal representatives present in the mediation room; privately paying clients will establish remuneration arrangements with their own solicitors.
- Legal representatives can be usefully involved for part only of the mediation process, especially towards the end – a helpful model is set out in an article by John Loram at (2008) 38 Fam Law 262.
- This is further explored in the wider context of the working partnerships between lawyers and mediators by Neil Robinson at [2008] Fam Law 1048, part of a series of articles about how the basic model of mediation can be further developed.

Shuttle mediation and caucusing

2.2.27   Although family mediation usually involves both parties meeting with the mediator at the same time, some mediators offer 'shuttle mediation' where the mediator shuttles between the parties who are each in separate rooms, most frequently with a view in due course to working together with the couple in the same room. However, some mediators take the view that if the parties never meet together it cannot be considered proper mediation.

2.2.28   The technique of caucusing, which is the norm in civil/commercial mediation, is another technique used by family mediators where the more standard mediation process seems to stall. Caucuses are meetings held by mediators separately with each side of a dispute, since without the presence of the other party, the party in caucus is likely to be less tense, angry and defensive, and more flexible and creative. Whereas in caucusing, mediators may hold secrets, particularly about parties' positions, shuttle mediation usually assumes that all information will be shared; that is, it is as if the parties are in the same room.

The benefits of mediation

2.2.29   Solicitors must explain to their clients the potential benefits of mediation. These include:

1.   When parties divorce or separate, it is generally better if both parties can sort out together their own practical arrangements for the future.

2. The aim of mediation is to help parties find a solution that meets the needs of all involved, especially any children, and that both parties feel is fair. At the end of mediation, those involved should feel that there has been no 'winner' or 'loser', but that together they have arrived at sensible, workable arrangements.

3. Mediation can help to reduce tension, hostility and misunderstandings and so improve communication between parties. This is especially important if children are involved as parties may need to cooperate over their care and upbringing for some years to come.

4. Mediation can offer general costs savings as parties have only one professional assisting them. It should also be noted, of course, that parties who are able to agree will incur lower fee levels.

5. Mediation has particular economic benefits where one or both parties are eligible for publicly funded family mediation since they will not be required to make any contribution towards the cost of the mediation, nor, often:

   (a) for the legal advice provided under public funding in connection with that mediation;

   (b) for the work involved in implementing the outcome of mediation into a court order by consent;

   (c) for any linked conveyancing required.

6. If a party is eligible for public funding for mediation then they will also be eligible for Level 2 Public Funding to pay for legal advice during the mediation, and for legal advice and legal implementation work at the end of the mediation.

7. Where a publicly funded matter can be settled in mediation the referring solicitor can claim the public funding settlement supplement.

8. Increasingly there is an expectation on the part of the family justice system that mediation will have been tried unless there are good reasons to the contrary.

The timing of the referral to mediation

2.2.30 It is important that solicitors should carefully consider and advise as to the timing of any referral to mediation.

2.2.31 In publicly funded cases there is a requirement to consider mediation no later than before Level 3 Public Funding or Legal Representation can be obtained. Where solicitors refer well before using up all available Level 2 funding it is possible to maximise financial return where settlement can be achieved in mediation with a minimal amount of support work from the solicitor.

2.2.32 However, even if the case is unsuitable for mediation at the outset, the possibility of a later referral should be kept under review as funding is available for such a later referral.

2.2.33 In private matters, the timing of the referral should be given especially careful consideration, depending on the facts of the case. For example, it may be appropriate to refer contact disputes to mediation as early as possible prior to the possibility of polarisation, whereas on financial matters it may sometimes be appropriate to deal with disclosure prior to such referral.

Supporting clients in mediation

Before mediation starts

2.2.34 Mediation works best when properly supported by independent legal advice. When referring clients to mediation, solicitors should explain that:

- they will support them in the mediation process with independent legal advice;
- public funding is available for those eligible;
- no financial agreement or other mediated outcome is directly binding between the parties without being approved by the court as a consent order or made legally binding in some other manner;
- they will advise as solicitors on the need and appropriateness of any such order;
- parties may consult their solicitors for advice, guidance and support at any stage during the mediation process, but that this is particularly important when disclosure and settlement proposals are being considered; and
- seeking such advice between mediation sessions can be positively helpful in establishing the appropriateness of proposals being discussed in mediation.

2.2.35 When referring a client to mediation a solicitor should, with the client's knowledge, forward to the mediator and provide a copy of the following (where available) to the other party's solicitors:

- any/all disclosure so far provided;
- a privileged summary of offers made;
- a privileged summary of areas of agreement and disagreement;
- where proceedings have been issued, a summary of the status of the case including details of orders made and any timetable given;
- details of other agencies already involved and the reasons for their involvement.

Whilst mediation is continuing

2.2.36 During mediation solicitors can usefully support clients with the following:

- assisting clients to provide disclosure where necessary and assess the disclosure which takes place in mediation (use of a Form E or Form E equivalent as a standard for disclosure in mediation is standard practice for many family mediators in England and Wales);
- giving advice about settlement proposals as and when required, bearing in mind the long-term interests of clients and/or of any children;
- offering and giving advice about other options;
- facilitating the obtaining of additional third-party input or information, for example welfare benefits advice (where not available directly from the solicitor's own firm) or expert valuation or accountancy advice;
- continuing to focus on the respective costs of mediation as opposed to mainstream legal proceedings, including, in particular the likely costs of court proceedings;
- supplying advice as to any untenable or unsustainable positions which either their client or the other party may be adopting;
- helping clients reach decisions;
- reminding clients to raise issues in mediation as appropriate;
- encouraging clients to 'stick with the process' unless inappropriate.

After mediation has concluded

2.2.37 Settlement proposals made in mediation are not binding between the parties. It is essential that legal advice is offered as to the merits of all and any proposals emerging from mediation as soon as they are available, and certainly before mediation concludes.

2.2.38 Following mediation, where parties are unable to reach firm proposals, solicitors should:

- discuss the reasons for the discontinuation of the mediation;
- note what has been achieved; and
- discuss what options for progression now arise.

2.2.39 Where the parties have produced interim proposals, discuss the position and any potential difficulties, including the need to apply for any interim orders.

2.2.40 Where proposals have been made, solicitors should follow the guidance in the main protocol (see **1.5.3**). Where it is appropriate to draft a consent order dealing with finances, the guidance on consent orders should be followed (see **3.6**).

2.3 COLLABORATIVE FAMILY LAW

Outline of collaborative family law

2.3.1 This is a process in which the solicitors and their clients agree in writing to reach a settlement without court involvement other than when processing the divorce papers and converting any agreement reached into a consent order. Both sets of solicitors and their clients agree to work together to resolve any issues to do with their children and the financial arrangements arising out of the breakdown in the relationship. As part of this team working, they may enlist other experts, such as children specialists or independent financial advisers.

2.3.2 This process is developing rapidly in the US and Canada and Resolution now trains collaborative lawyers in England and Wales, also prescribing standards and materials for use in the collaborative process. Limited public funding is, in the near future, expected to be made available for collaborative law.

2.3.3 The main cornerstone of the collaborative process is the exclusion clause in the participation agreement. Once signed, if either party decides to commence court proceedings both lawyers must withdraw and new solicitors will be appointed by both clients.

2.3.4 Collaborative family lawyers will have undergone training through Resolution in collaborative principles and techniques. These will include client representation, negotiation and problem solving. The process is centred on a series of 'four-way' meetings attended by both clients and their lawyers and any other experts that have been enlisted. During these meetings they will seek to shape a fair agreement.

2.3.5 As with mediation, the discussions will be carried out through 'interest-based' rather than 'positional' bargaining, placing the balancing of the competing interests of the various family members at the heart of the negotiations.

2.3.6 Where full agreement cannot be reached, and one or other client decides to seek the involvement of the courts, both solicitors must withdraw from the process and each of the clients will need to instruct new firms of solicitors to proceed conventionally.

Screening for collaborative cases

2.3.7   As with mediation, it is important that only cases which are suitable are offered the collaborative process.

2.3.8   Many of the considerations set out in **2.2.8–2.2.11** above may also apply. However, as one of the principles of collaborative practice is that the process can proceed at the pace with which both parties feel most comfortable, in cases where counselling or marital therapy might be suitable, this can be factored in to the process structure.

Advising clients about the collaborative option

2.3.9   At an early stage solicitors must, unless it is clearly inappropriate to do so, explain the collaborative process and advise clients as to the benefits (including the benefits as to costs and as to timescale) and/or limitations of collaboration in their particular case. Where the solicitor is not personally collaboratively trained, the client should be advised of this and as to the options available.

2.3.10   Where a collaboratively trained solicitor, on first instruction, considers that a case may be suitable for the collaborative process, the solicitor should advise his client of this, and also that it will be a matter for their spouse or former partner whether they instruct a collaboratively trained lawyer or not. If appropriate, the solicitor can provide to the party a list of local collaboratively trained lawyers.

The benefits of collaborative practice

2.3.11   Solicitors must explain to their clients the potential benefits of the collaborative process. These include:

1.   When parties divorce or separate, it is generally better if both parties can sort out together their own practical arrangements for the future.
2.   The aim of the collaborative process is to help parties find a solution that meets the needs of all involved, especially any children, and that both parties feel is fair. At the end of the collaborative process, those involved should feel that there has been no 'winner' or 'loser', but that together they have arrived at sensible, workable arrangements.
3.   Collaboration can help to reduce tension, hostility and misunderstandings and so improve communication between parties. This is especially important if children are involved as parties may need to cooperate over their care and upbringing for some years to come.

4. Collaboration may offer costs savings as against a fully litigated case. It is not cheaper than mediation.

5. As part of the process, agreement is reached at an early stage as to responsibility for meeting the legal costs for both parties to ensure a level playing field.

6. The process is unique in its potential for involvement of other experts within and supporting the negotiations.

7. Unlike mediation, the lawyer is present at, and supportive during, the negotiations.

8. Once agreement has been reached there is no reference back to any other adviser for further advice.

2.3.12 Collaborative law has many benefits as regards the management and in particular the emotional management of the parties to the dispute. There may not be significant costs savings as between the collaborative law process and the conventional process of settlement by inter-solicitor negotiation.

2.3.13 Collaborative law is one of a developing range of services to assist clients to resolve issues without the need for court proceedings. As with mediation, it will not be suitable for everyone, but is a useful process for some couples and may help them to manage relationship breakdown more easily.

2.4 ROUTES INTO ADR?

2.4.1 The available mechanisms for diversion of contesting participants away from litigation into mediation (if not into additional forms of ADR), tallied against those who have capacity to effect such diversion, are set out in the following Table.

	Party/ Parties	Solicitor(s)	Court Admin	Judge/Legal Adviser
Self referral	Yes*			
Law Society Protocol	Yes*	Yes*		
LSC Funding Code		Yes		
Compulsory consideration of mediation		Possible?	Yes	
External court referral (referral out)			Yes	Yes
In-court mediation referral				Yes
Contact activity direction				Yes

*These referral mechanisms and referrers also have the capacity to effect referrals to ADR processes other than mediation. The mechanism identified in italics is at the date of writing currently under ministerial consideration, but expected to be introduced from April 2011.

PART 3

Agreements

3.1 SCOPE

3.1.1 Clients are increasingly anxious to provide certainty for the future by entering into agreements with their partners. This is, however, an area of law fraught with risk. The extent to which agreements can be enforced depends on the type of agreement and how it has been prepared. The difficulty in advising clients is increased by the uncertainty as we await the judgement of the Supreme Court in the appeal against the decision in *Radmacher* v. *Granatino* [2009] EWCA Civ 649 [AQ]. In the meantime solicitors must ensure that the appropriate procedures are followed and that clear advice is given as to the limitations and risks involved in such agreements.

3.2 PRE-NUPTIAL AGREEMENTS

3.2.1 This is an agreement entered into by a couple before their marriage or civil partnership which seeks to prescribe what should happen in the event that their relationship breaks down.

3.2.2 Pre-nuptial agreements are not currently enforceable under English law. They are, however, a circumstance of the case which the courts are required to consider pursuant to the Matrimonial Causes Act (MCA) 1973, s.25. The courts have recently given increasing weight to pre-nuptial agreements in ancillary relief proceedings and solicitors advising on pre-nuptial agreements must be familiar with the decisions in *Radmacher* v. *Granatino*, *MacLeod* v. *MacLeod* [2008] UKPC 64 and *Crossley* v. *Crossley* [2007] EWCA Civ 1491.

3.2.3 The Court of Appeal in *Crossley* v. *Crossley* confirmed that the existence of a pre-nuptial agreement could not oust the court's obligation to apply MCA 1973, s.25. They said, however, that in this case the agreement was 'a factor of magnetic importance'. They upheld the trial judge's approach which they stated to be in accordance with a developing view that pre-nuptial contracts were growing in importance. It should be borne in mind that this was a short, childless marriage with substantial wealth on both sides.

3.2.4   *MacLeod* v. *MacLeod* concerned a wealthy American couple living in the Isle of Man. They executed a pre-nuptial agreement which was reviewed twice during the marriage. A post-nuptial agreement was subsequently drawn up confirming the terms of the pre-nuptial agreement with some amendments. The Privy Council distinguished between agreements entered into before and after marriage, finding that the latter could be binding if properly executed. The Privy Council was at pains to state in this case, however, that for reasons of public policy pre-nuptial agreements are not contractually binding. Practice has developed as a consequence that both may be prepared at the same time with the post-nuptial agreement, confirming the terms of the pre-nuptial agreement, being executed after the wedding.

3.2.5   In *Radmacher* v. *Granatino* the Court of Appeal suggested that so long as the court retained ultimate discretion pursuant to MCA 1973, s.25 there was no need for such concerns of public policy. The Court of Appeal's judgment emphasised the need for England to move with the times and stated that it was increasingly unrealistic not to recognise properly negotiated pre nuptial agreements. In giving weight to the pre-nuptial agreement the Court of Appeal considered it important that the parties in this case were from France and Germany where pre-marital agreements are standard practice and enforceable. The Court of Appeal did not consider that the husband's decision not to take legal advice or negotiate made the agreement void. He was a man of the world and aware of his wife's wealth.

3.2.6   The decision of the Supreme Court in respect of *Radmacher* v. *Granatino* is expected in October 2010 and it is hoped will offer solicitors further guidance as to the status of pre-nuptial and other agreements.

3.2.7   The weight attached to a pre-nuptial agreement will be affected by the way it has been negotiated and drafted. The following points should be considered:

- Both parties should take independent legal advice before entering into the agreement. This should be recorded on the face of the agreement.
- The agreement should be entered into voluntarily and neither party must exploit a dominant position.
- The requirement for each party to take independent advice may also apply to experts, for example an accountant or financial adviser. That such advice has been taken should also be set out in the agreement.

- Both parties should provide full and frank disclosure before signing the agreement. This should be attached to the agreement and contain details as to income, assets/liabilities and pension provision. The more comprehensive the information produced the more weight that is likely to be given to the agreement.
- The agreement should be signed well before the marriage, i.e. at least more than 21 days. This will help to avoid suggestion of duress.
- The agreement should set out:
  - that the parties intend to create a legally binding contract;
  - that there would have been no marriage without the agreement;
  - how all assets are to be divided, including pre-marital and post-separation accruals;
  - what should happen in the case of a change in circumstance, e.g. the birth of a child.
- The more even handed the terms the more weight the agreement is likely to be given by the court.
- The Resolution publication, *Separation, Pre-Marriage and Pre-Civil Partnership Agreements* (2008) contains invaluable precedents for the drafting of pre-nuptial agreements.

3.2.8 Clients should be advised to enter into a post-nuptial agreement ratifying the terms of the pre-nuptial agreement for the reasons set out at **3.4**.

3.3   MAINTENANCE AGREEMENTS

3.3.1 Despite their name, maintenance agreements are not limited to periodical payments. A maintenance agreement is any agreement made in writing during the marriage or after its dissolution which contains financial arrangements. It can deal, therefore, with the treatment of any assets and provision for spousal or child maintenance.

3.3.2 Separation agreements need not contain financial provision and can deal solely with the separation. The agreement can be evidence that the marriage was considered at an end for the purposes of divorce or judicial separation proceedings.

3.3.3 MCA 1973, s.34 makes maintenance agreements binding on the parties although s.35 gives the court the power to vary such agreements where:

- there has been a change in circumstance – even if foreseeable; or
- it fails to provide for a child; or
- the terms require the state to support someone who should be supported by the family.

3.3.4   Post-nuptial agreements and separation agreements may constitute maintenance agreements, although these are very rarely used in practice.

3.4   POST-NUPTIAL AGREEMENTS

3.4.1   These are agreements made between the parties prior to separation setting out how they would wish matters to be resolved in the event of a separation. The contents are, therefore, likely to be similar to that of a pre-nuptial agreement and consideration should be given to the guidance on negotiation and drafting at **3.2.7**.

3.4.2   In *MacLeod* v. *MacLeod* (above), the Privy Council drew a firm distinction between pre-nuptial and post-nuptial agreements, finding the latter to be binding upon the parties as a maintenance agreement pursuant to MCA 1973, s.34.

3.4.3   Given the courts power to vary such agreements pursuant to MCA 1973, s.35 in the event of a change in circumstance, clients should be advised to review and ratify the terms of their post-nuptial agreements on a regular basis.

3.4.4   Solicitors should advise clients of the uncertainty created in respect of post-nuptial agreements by the Court of Appeal in *Radmacher* v. *Granatino* when Wilson LJ referred to MCA 1973, ss.34 and 35 as being 'dead letters' and failed to make any distinction between pre- and post-nuptial agreements. It is hoped that the Supreme Court will address this in their judgment.

3.5   SEPARATION AGREEMENTS

3.5.1   Separation agreements regulate the position when spouses separate but do not wish to embark on divorce proceedings. They can be useful, therefore, if parties wish to divorce on grounds of separation but wish to formalise their financial arrangements in the interim or do not want to divorce for religious or cultural reasons.

3.5.2   The contents of such agreements can be very flexible, dealing with:

- maintenance (child or spousal);
- property/assets;
- arrangements for children;
- practicalities of the separation.

3.5.3 Although *MacLeod* v. *MacLeod* did not specifically deal with separation agreements, it dealt with agreements between parties to a marriage and it must follow, therefore, that a separation agreement may be binding as a maintenance agreement pursuant to MCA 1973, s.34, subject to the comments in *Radmacher* v. *Granatino*.

3.5.4 The guidance at **3.2.7** is equally applicable to separation agreements.

3.5.5 Clients must be advised that a separation agreement may not oust the jurisdiction of the court and that it does not preclude an application for ancillary relief in the future by their spouse.

3.6 CONSENT ORDERS

3.6.1 Where parties have agreed the terms of a financial settlement this should usually be drawn up into a consent order and submitted to the court for approval.

3.6.2 When drafting a consent order solicitors must ensure that the main body of the order contains only provisions which the court has power to make pursuant to MCA 1973, ss.23, 24, 24A, 24B, 25B and 25C. Other matters on which the parties have agreed should be dealt with as recitals and/or undertakings. The form of such undertakings differs between courts with some insisting that undertakings be given between the parties rather than to the court. Resolution's *Precedents for Consent Orders* (now in its 8th edition) is an extremely useful resource when drafting such orders.

3.6.3 If the consent order has been agreed at a hearing the judge will normally approve it immediately, having been provided with a signed form of wording.

3.6.4 A consent order can, however, be submitted to court for consideration by a judge without the need for attendance. The following must be included:

- the draft consent order signed by both parties and their solicitors;
- three perfected copies for sealing, leaving blank the date and name of judge;
- a Form M1 Statement of Information containing the information prescribed by the Family Proceedings Rules (FPR) 1991, SI 1991/ 1247, rule 2.61: both parties' details can be included on the same form or alternatively two separate documents submitted;
- a £40 fee will be payable unless ancillary relief proceedings have already been issued;

- a Form A required by some courts marked 'for dismissal purposes only': if ancillary relief proceedings have been issued this will only be required from the respondent to those proceedings.

3.6.5 If one or both of the parties is acting in person the court may direct a short hearing before approving the terms of the consent order to satisfy itself in particular that there is no duress and that everyone is aware of the binding nature of the terms.

3.6.6 Once approved by the court a consent order generally constitutes a full and final settlement of financial claims. The exceptions are where there has been material non-disclosure or a *Barder* event (see **3.6.8**).

3.6.7 A consent order may be set aside if one party has failed to provide full and frank disclosure. The non-disclosure must be material so that it would have made a substantial difference to the order the court would have made. Non-disclosure itself is insufficient to justify a review.

3.6.8 *Barder* v. *Barder* [1988] AC 20 established that an order, including a consent order, could be appealed where:

- new events have occurred which invalidate the basis on which the order was made;
- these new events occurred within a relatively short time of the order being made (generally less than one year);
- leave to appeal is made promptly;
- third parties acting in good faith will not be prejudiced.

The new event must not be ordinary, natural, or foreseeable. A change of value will rarely be a *Barder* event unless there has been a mistake.

3.7 UNPERFECTED ORDERS (ROSE AGREEMENTS)

3.7.1 At a financial dispute resolution (FDR) hearing when the terms of a financial settlement have been agreed it is not always possible to place a final consent order before the judge for approval. This may be because there is insufficient time for detailed drafting or that formal requirements need to be completed, e.g. serving the pension trustees.

3.7.2 In such cases the judge can still be invited to approve the terms which have been agreed. That agreement will then be upheld as an order of the court.

3.7.3 The status of these agreements was considered in the case of *Rose* v. *Rose* [2002] 1 FLR 978 in which a husband attempted to withdraw from the terms of an agreement approved at an FDR hearing but not drawn up into a consent order. The Court of Appeal held that an unperfected order had been entered into and could not be set aside.

3.8 AGREEMENTS PRIOR TO FINAL ORDER (XYDHIAS AGREEMENTS)

3.8.1 This is an agreement reached as to the terms of a financial settlement which has not been made into a final order. The agreement may be contained in solicitors' correspondence, heads of agreement or a draft consent order.

3.8.2 In the case of *Xydhias* v. *Xydhias* [1999] 1 FLR 683, an agreement had been negotiated between a husband and wife and several draft consent orders produced. The husband then withdrew all offers and stated that he wished to proceed to a contested hearing. The wife applied for an order that the husband show cause why an order should not be made in the terms agreed. The district judge found that there had been a concluded agreement. The Court of Appeal gave the following points of guidance which must be considered by a solicitor asked to advise on whether such an agreement exists:

- An agreement to compromise an ancillary relief claim is not enforceable in law.
- If there is a dispute as to whether an accord has been reached, the court has the discretion to decide applying the MCA 1973, s.25 factors and considering vitiating factors such as material non-disclosure or duress.
- Ordinarily heads of agreement (as distinct from a draft of the consent order) signed by the parties or a clear exchange of solicitors' letters will establish the necessary consensus.
- It is good practice to have the parties and counsel sign heads of agreement setting out in simple terms what the applicant will receive.

3.8.3 If there is a dispute as to whether a *Xydhias* agreement has been reached then the party who asserts that the agreement has been made should apply to the court for this preliminary issue to be determined. If there are no existing proceedings such application would be by way of Form A.

3.9 COHABITATION AGREEMENTS

3.9.1 These are entered into by couples who are either living together but are not married, or are in a civil partnership, in order to regulate their affairs during and/or after separation.

3.9.2   Properly concluded cohabitation agreements will be binding (*Sutton* v. *Mishcon de Reya* [2004] 1 FLR 837). The extent to which a cohabitation agreement will be enforced will depend on the contents and how it has been negotiated.

3.9.3   The terms of the agreement can be very flexible. Some suggestions as to issues which should be included are as follows:

- **Outgoings** – who is to be responsible both pre- and post-separation.
- **Property** – how this is owned to include the defining of beneficial interests. How it should be treated on separation. Contributions to upkeep/maintenance.
- **Joint accounts** – contributions and restrictions on spending.
- **Assets** – ownership and entitlement on separation in relation to cars, furniture and other property.
- **Debt** – who is to be responsible during the relationship and on separation.
- **Maintenance** – will any be payable on separation?
- **Financial provision for children** – including maintenance and school fees.

3.9.4   *Precedents for Cohabitation Agreements*, published by Resolution (2006), provides many more suggestions as to areas which should be considered and guidance on drafting.

3.10   PARENTAL RESPONSIBILITY AGREEMENTS

3.10.1   If a father is not married to the mother of his child at the time of that child's birth he does not automatically have parental responsibility. If the child was born before 1 December 2003, the father may only obtain parental responsibility either by a parental responsibility agreement or by an order of the court. If the child was born after 1 December 2003 and the father is named on the birth certificate he automatically obtains parental responsibility. If he is not so named he will similarly need either a parental responsibility agreement or court order.

3.10.2   The agreement must be in the prescribed form (Form C(PRA1)) which can be found on the court service website (**www.hmcourts-service.gov.uk**).

3.10.3   The form sets out detailed information as to its completion. The child's mother and father must attend at court, either separately or together, and sign the agreement in the presence of a court official authorised to administer oaths. They must have proof of identification and the mother must have the child's full birth certificate.

3.10.4   Once signed, the original and two copies of the agreement should be sent to the Principal Registry in London. The mother and father will each receive a sealed copy of the agreement and a copy will be retained by the court.

3.11   PARENTING AGREEMENTS/PLANS

3.11.1   This is a document drawn up by parents who are separating, or have separated, setting out what they have agreed in respect of arrangements for their children. The agreement is not binding and cannot be enforced by a court. The contents could, however, be brought to the court's attention in future proceedings in relation to such arrangements.

3.11.2   Parents should be encouraged to enter into parenting agreements, no matter how informal the document. A parenting plan requires parents to address issues involving their children and to reach agreement as to how they should be managed. This will help to avoid conflict or misunderstanding in the future and the children will have certainty and the knowledge that their parents have worked together to agree what is best for them.

3.11.3   The following are just some of the issues which could be included in a parenting plan/agreement:

- How will the children be told about the separation and the arrangements which have been made for them?
- How will the children share their time between their parents?
- What will happen if arrangements need to be changed?
- Is anyone else going to be involved in their care (childminders, family members, etc.)?
- Will there be phone calls or other communications between parents/children?
- Are there any particular rules which must apply in both homes, e.g. bedtime?
- Introduction of new partners.
- School holiday arrangements.
- Where should passports be kept?
- What should happen if the children are ill?

3.11.4   Solicitors can refer their clients to an excellent booklet written by Cafcass: *Parenting Plans: Putting Your Children First – A Guide for Separating Parents* (which can be downloaded free of charge from **www.cafcass. gov.uk**). This contains further ideas as to what could be included in such agreements and general guidance for separating parents. See also 'Parenting after Parting' (available at **www.resolution.org.uk**).

3.12   CHILD MAINTENANCE AGREEMENTS

3.12.1   This is a contractual agreement between the parents of a child which provides for the maintenance and support of that child.

3.12.2   It is preferable for such an agreement to be in the form of a deed. This avoids the need for the person seeking to enforce its terms to prove good consideration.

3.12.3   If the agreement was made on or after 5 April 1993 then either party can still apply to the Child Support Agency (CSA) for an assessment. If it pre-dates 5 April 1993 then no application can be made to the CSA.

PART 4

Domestic abuse

Solicitors should keep under review at all times the availability of public funding and its extended availability in cases of domestic violence and the need to provide clients with costs information at the outset and on a regular basis.

4.1 BEFORE THE ISSUE OF AN INJUNCTION APPLICATION

What is domestic abuse?

4.1.1 Domestic abuse has not been defined in law in England and Wales. Whether domestic abuse has occured is decided in any given case on the evidence presented to the court. The Inter-Ministerial Group on Domestic Violence signed up to the following definition of domestic abuse in 2004:

> Any incident of threatening behaviour, violence or abuse (psychological, physical, sexual, financial or emotional) between adults who are or have been intimate partners or family members, regardless of gender or sexuality.

4.1.2 An adult is defined as any person aged 18 and over. Family members are defined as mother, father, son, daughter, brother, sister and grandparents, whether directly related, in-laws or step-family.

4.1.3 Practitioners are referred to the Family Law Act (FLA) 1996 as extended by the Domestic Violence, Crime and Victims Act 2004. Under those Acts a 'domestic relationship' includes partners, family members and 'associated persons' as defined in FLA 1996. This was extended by the Domestic Violence, Crime and Victims Act 2004 to include cousins, same-sex cohabitants and those who have been in an intimate personal relationship of a significant duration.

4.1.4 Domestic abuse can include:

(a) physical abuse, including slapping, pushing and physical intimidation generally;

(b) sexual abuse, including female genital mutilation;

33

(c)   psychological abuse, including but not limited to:

   (i)   intimidation;
   (ii)   harassment;
   (iii) damage to property;
   (iv)   threats of physical, sexual or psychological abuse;
   (v)   controlling behaviour, including financial abuse and isolation of a victim;

(d)   forced marriage, which may include elements of (a) and (c);

(e)   in relation to a child, causing them to witness or putting them at risk of witnessing the abuse of a person with whom they have a domestic relationship (this does not apply to the person who suffers the abuse).

4.1.5   Domestic abuse may be a single act or a number of acts forming a pattern of behaviour, even though some or all of these acts when viewed in isolation may appear to be minor or trivial.

4.1.6   Domestic abuse is a controlling, coercive pattern of behaviour that often goes on for an extended period of time. Although individual acts may appear minor or trivial when viewed in isolation, it is the overall effect on the victim and any children that needs to be considered.

4.1.7   Forced marriage is a specific form of domestic abuse and solicitors should be aware of it and screen for it.

4.1.8   When dealing with clients who have been the victims of forced marriage, solicitors who do not have experience of advising on this issue should refer any clients to another solicitor or organisation who has experience in advising as to the parties' rights under FLA 1996, Part IVA, which was introduced by the Forced Marriage (Civil Protection) Act 2007. The purpose of a forced marriage protection order is to protect a person from being forced into marriage or from any attempt to do so, or to protect a person who has already been forced into a marriage and to remove him/her from that situation. Currently there are only 14 designated courts having jurisdiction to hear any such applications across England and Wales. Solicitors should enquire as to the nearest available court and refer any person who may be the victim of a forced marriage to specialist advice.

Screening for domestic abuse

4.1.9   The role of solicitors in identifying domestic abuse can be invaluable. In order to respond more effectively to domestic abuse, solicitors should:

- recognise that domestic abuse is a serious problem, and always prioritise the safety of victims. It is important not to collude with perpetrators;
- recognise that domestic abuse occurs irrespective of class, race or
  ethnicity, sex or sexuality, age, mental or physical ability, and be
  sensitive to different needs and experiences of clients from different
  backgrounds and cultures;
- ask questions about domestic abuse directly and routinely as part of
  normal interview procedures. Solicitors should be aware that disclosure may be piecemeal and so questions should be asked sensitively
  and appropriately at each interview;
- not be judgemental;
- have information about other sources of help and support available
  within the local area and keep such information up to date.

4.1.10   The Resolution Domestic Abuse Screening Toolkit has contact details for
some of the organisations that can provide help and advice. A copy can be
downloaded from **www.resolution.org.uk**. For other resources see the list
at **Appendix A**.

Screening questions

4.1.11   Impartial screening techniques should be used as part of normal interview
techniques to establish if there is an issue of domestic abuse for that
individual client. Solicitors must recognise that victims may not disclose
domestic abuse at first or early meetings. Screening questions might
include:

1. Have you been arguing a lot recently?
2. Do you generally have a lot of arguments?
3. When you argue, what usually happens?
4. Have you or your partner ever been convicted of any criminal
   offence, in particular those including violence and/or drugs or alcohol?
5. What happens when your partner loses their temper and/or you lose
   your temper?
6. When you and/or your partner drink alcohol does this ever result in
   arguments?
7. Do you and/or your partner ever become violent after consuming
   alcohol or any other substance?
8. How safe or afraid do you and/or your partner feel in your current
   relationship?
9. Has your partner ever threatened you with a weapon and have you
   ever threatened him or her with a weapon?

> 10. Has your partner threatened to harm himself or herself and/or the children and have you ever threatened to harm yourself and/or the children?
> 11. Has your partner ever stalked you and have you ever stalked your partner?

4.1.12 Whether to raise the issue of possible domestic abuse with a client who may be a perpetrator is obviously a very sensitive matter. Where there are children of the family, any screening which is carried out must seek to establish whether there is an issue of abuse for the client only or for the client and any children of the family. Where there are children of the family, screening needs to include questions about the client's own propensity. This is the reason why the questions above are drafted to include the conduct of both parties.

4.1.13 If solicitors suspect that their client is the victim of domestic abuse, more direct questions should be considered, for example:

> 1. Are you afraid of your partner?
> 2. Why are you afraid of him or her?
> 3. Has there ever been any violence between you?
> 4. Have either of you been hurt by the other? If so, is the violence escalating in frequency and/or severity?
> 5. Were these injuries caused by someone you know?
> 6. Have your children ever witnessed any violence between you?
> 7. Are you/is your partner currently pregnant?
> 8. Do you have any disabilities (mental or physical)?
> 9. What support networks do you have in terms of friends, family or others?

These questions are based on National Family Mediation guidelines for screening for domestic abuse in mediation, but have been revised and extended after consultation. Note that these questions are not exhaustive and they do not represent a comprehensive list.

4.1.14 Even where domestic abuse does not emerge as an issue at the initial interview, the possibility of abuse should be kept under review at all times.

Needs assessment

4.1.15 If domestic abuse does emerge as an issue, solicitors will need, as appropriate, to do the following:

> 1. Explain the options available if clients want to take any action, ensuring the victim's safety is paramount throughout while accepting that clients must be allowed to make their own decisions.

2. Advise on the strengths and limitations of each remedy in curbing the abuse and the potential impact on the abuser of any possible course of action.

3. Advise on the prospects of obtaining an order and the merits, implications and costs of the remedies.

4. Discuss the potential impact of the domestic abuse on any children, including potential risks involved when considering contact arrangements and the likely effect upon them of any action clients wish to take.

5. Discuss whether any application needs to be made to protect the children of the family or any one of them.

6. Discuss how a partner's abuse will impact on other legal remedies or proceedings such as divorce, residence, contact, ancillary relief and immigration.

7. Provide information about other agencies and support groups as appropriate.

8. Give assistance, where appropriate and where possible, with the practical problems posed by domestic abuse. For example:

   (a) discuss appropriate safe contact telephone numbers and addresses;

   (b) discuss keeping a log of any incidents which arise if it is safe to do so;

   (c) discuss keeping certain documents in solicitors' offices, for example passports, health cards, bank documents and children's photographs.

9. Consider with clients whether it is appropriate to change the numbers of their mobile and home telephones.

10. Discuss safety planning and if appropriate prepare an action plan for clients. An action plan can be found in the LSC's leaflet on domestic violence and harassment (**www.communitylegaladvice.org.uk**).

11. Suggest to clients that they telephone the police when incidents occur and ask the police to log these incidents and give clients the relevant log number.

12. Advise as to the recording of evidence including photographs of injuries, dated where possible.

Compiling a record of evidence

Gathering evidence

4.1.16   Solicitors should discuss with clients the need to protect existing evidence of violence or harassment and the need to think about gathering evidence in the future. This may be particularly important where a client has an insecure immigration status and wishes to apply for indefinite leave to remain in the UK under the 'domestic violence rule' within immigration law.

4.1.17   Actions to produce a record of the abuse may include:

- urging clients to visit their GPs to have a record made of any injuries;
- advising clients to obtain photographs of any injuries immediately after any violent episode or when any bruising develops (preferably with some evidence of the date on which the photographs were taken);
- asking clients for the names and addresses of any witnesses to the violence or harassment and taking statements from them, or asking the client to obtain written statements from them;
- encouraging clients to keep a diary or record of events which has been contemporaneously signed and dated;
- asking clients to retain abusive or threatening notes, e-mails or other written communications;
- asking clients to keep photocopies of abusive or threatening text messages and to record abusive or threatening telephone messages.

Personal statements

4.1.18   Solicitors should consider and discuss with clients the benefits of making personal statements, and where appropriate assist clients to do so. Local domestic abuse support services may also be able to assist with this, and provide follow-up support once the personal statement has been made. A personal statement is a short document, possibly in letter form, setting out a client's statement of the domestic abuse which they state they have suffered. Solicitors should recognise that some domestic abuse sufferers will need follow-up support after outlining the history of the abuse they have suffered. This can be used to provide information to other agencies from which services or support may be needed, for example the Department for Work and Pensions. Clients should be advised that statements may be given to those agencies and that it may be necessary for them to confirm their position verbally to other agencies.

4.1.19   Preparation of such a statement should avoid the need for the client to tell the same story in full to a number of different agencies, although further details may be required by those agencies. For the statements to be of use they will need to be regularly updated. Clients should be advised that the confidentiality of such statements cannot be guaranteed once they have been given to other agencies.

Safety planning

4.1.20   As soon as domestic abuse is revealed as an issue, solicitors should prioritise the safety of clients and any children and advise clients as to how to protect themselves and their children. The following matters should be considered.

Confidentiality

4.1.21   Solicitors should discuss with clients their duty of confidentiality and the opportunity to speak openly without fear of disclosure. However, it is very important to explain clearly the limits of that confidentiality, particularly in relation to the court's powers to order disclosure of information about the whereabouts of a child. It should also be made clear that the duty of confidentiality does not extend to information about the commission of a crime, including child abduction, or about harm or the threat of harm to a child (for guidance on this, contact the Professional Ethics department at the Solicitors Regulation Authority (see **Appendix B**)). Solicitors should also consider the guidance given in Rule 4 of the Solicitors' Code of Conduct 2007.

Keeping clients' whereabouts confidential

4.1.22   When clients are in hiding or face particular risk from their partners or families, solicitors should discuss with them the possible dangers of disclosure of their whereabouts once proceedings are issued. Solicitors need to consider carefully whether injunctive relief is appropriate in such circumstances.

4.1.23   Solicitors should consider ways in which clients' whereabouts can be kept confidential, such as:

- issuing proceedings in a different location (although it will be necessary to explain to clients that there will be an increase in costs as a result of using agents);
- asking the court for leave to withhold clients' addresses from documentation;
- the use of agent solicitors in a different area of the country;
- constant vigilance about the contents of documents;
- rules about the posting of letters and documents.

4.1.24   However, solicitors should advise clients of the court's powers under FLA 1986, s.33 in relation to disclosure of the whereabouts of a child to the court.

Sources of funding

4.1.25   The upper income and capital limits can be waived to enable a domestic abuse sufferer to have public funding for an injunction application, but contributions from income and capital still apply. Where the domestic abuse sufferer does not want to pay the contribution or to pay privately for the cost of legal advice and obtaining protection, solicitors should provide information about other sources of help to obtain protection through the courts. For contact details of these organisations see **Appendix B**.

Criminal proceedings

4.1.26   Solicitors should consider whether it is more appropriate for a client for the incidents to be dealt with in the criminal court as a crime. If so, it is important to liaise with the police. The police will investigate any offence reported and then, in all but the most minor and straightforward cases, refer the case to the Crown Prosecution Service (CPS) which will determine whether a person is to be charged. If an offence investigated by the police is classified as 'domestic violence' the charging decision must always be made by the CPS. Domestic abuse cases may involve many different criminal offences, most commonly assault. A prosecution can be brought under the Protection from Harassment Act 1997 where there has been a course of conduct of harassment. However, solicitors should bear in mind that the burden of proof in criminal proceedings under the Protection from Harassment Act 1997 is proof beyond reasonable doubt, as opposed to proof on the balance of probabilities in civil proceedings either under that Act or under FLA 1996, Part IV. Solicitors should be aware that an application for an injunction under the Protection from Harassment Act 1997, s.3 may be founded on the basis of one act of harassment and anticipated further breaches of s.1. In contrast a prosecution under s.2 or s.4 of the Act requires at least two actual incidents in order to constitute 'a course of conduct'.

4.1.27   Solicitors should be aware of the differences between criminal and civil proceedings under the Protection from Harassment Act 1997 and potential disadvantages to the client in relying on criminal sanctions (see **4.1.28**).

4.1.28   Solicitors should bear in mind that in criminal proceedings (including prosecution for breach of a non-molestation order) there are certain advantages and disadvantages for the domestic abuse sufferer.

4.1.29   On conviction or acquittal of any offence the court can impose a restraining order of any duration to restrain further harassment (Domestic Violence,

Crime and Victims Act 2004, s.12). Orders on acquittal may be made where it is clear from the evidence that a victim needs some form of protection.

Family Law Act 1996, Part IV: clients under an incapacity

4.1.30   Solicitors are reminded that any child applicant for an injunction under FLA 1996 must proceed by a next friend. Unless they are particularly complex, proceedings must commence in the county court. In addition, any child under 16 needs the leave of the court to issue an application (FLA 1996, s.43). Rule 9.2A of the Family Proceedings Rules (FPR) 1991, SI 1991/1247 does not apply (FPR 1991, rule 9.2, and see rule 9.1(3)). Any child respondent for a Family Law Act injunction must proceed by guardian ad litem (FPR 1991, rule 9.2 and rule 9.1(3)). The Official Solicitor will act as next friend or guardian ad litem of the minor if there is no other suitable person to do so. Solicitors should be aware that remedies against minors are limited (FLA 1996, s.47(2); *H* v. *H (A Child) (Occupation Order: Power of Arrest)* [2001] 1 FLR 641; Powers of Criminal Courts (Sentencing) Act 2000, s.89(1)). However, now that breach of a non-molestation order is a criminal offence it should be possible to obtain a non-molestation order against a minor who is old enough to be prosecuted for breach.

4.1.31   Clients who are patients as defined by the Mental Capacity Act 2005 must begin proceedings by a next friend and defend proceedings by a guardian ad litem (FPR 1991, rule 9.1(1) and rule 9.2). Solicitors are reminded that a potential contemnor must be able to understand that an order has been made forbidding him or her to do certain things and that if he or she does them they will be punished (*P* v. *P (Contempt of Court: Mental Capacity)* [1999] 2 FLR 897, together with the earlier case of *Wookey* v. *Wookey* [1991] 2 FLR 319).

4.2   SERVICE OF NOTICE

Service of papers

4.2.1   Solicitors should ask the court to return issued papers to them immediately so that they can arrange service on respondents. Solicitors can then arrange for personal service of these documents or, if permitted, by some other means. If the client is taking divorce proceedings, solicitors should consider serving the divorce documents with the injunction application in order to minimise cost and delay. Solicitors should forewarn clients when papers are due to be served as they may need to leave the home or take other steps to protect themselves.

4.2.2 Solicitors are referred to Resolution's *Guide to Good Practice on Service* (see **Appendix A**).

Leaving the home

4.2.3 If clients are still living with violent partners, solicitors should discuss with clients whether they need to leave their home before service of proceedings.

4.2.4 If so, or if clients are considering leaving the family home in any event, temporarily or permanently, it is important to discuss the implications of this action and the effect it may have on the children, including financial aspects. Solicitors should advise clients of the support available from women's refuges.

4.2.5 Solicitors should also discuss with clients the need to take with them irreplaceable and important items such as photographs, legal documents, personal items of monetary or sentimental value, passports and benefit entitlement documents.

4.2.6 Solicitors should discuss the possibility of clients returning home with police assistance to collect their belongings if the police are willing and able to assist.

4.2.7 Solicitors should, however, warn clients that they should not take joint or similarly classed items or strip the house of contents or behave in any other highly inflammatory manner.

4.2.8 Solicitors must advise clients that if they leave their children with their partners they must not assume that the children will be returned to them automatically by the court. The police are unlikely to assist in retrieving children unless they are perceived to be 'at risk' and former partners may be unwilling to relinquish them.

Other proceedings, negotiations and hearings

4.2.9 Where domestic abuse is an issue, great care should be taken to ensure that a client's safety is not compromised by meetings arranged by third parties (for example, the Cafcass officer) and that clients are not pressured into face-to-face meetings with their ex-partners for the purposes of 'door of the court' negotiations on, for example, children or financial matters. Safety issues should be raised with Cafcass officers if they are or become involved.

4.2.10 Any safety issues within the confines of the court building should be discussed with court staff in advance. Where necessary an application should be made for special measures such as giving evidence via video link from another location or from behind a screen in the courtroom.

4.3 INJUNCTION PROCEEDINGS

4.3.1 Solicitors should ensure that the process of obtaining legal protection for parties who are or have been the victims of domestic abuse is as supportive, effective and as fast as possible.

4.3.2 Solicitors should not accept instructions in a domestic abuse case unless they have time, expertise and capacity to deal with it speedily and to give the client the time they may require.

4.3.3 Where a client is referred by the National Centre for Domestic Violence, or any other organisation which prepares a statement for the client, the solicitor should ensure that they have full instructions.

4.3.4 The proposed proceedings should be discussed with all clients before issue. The client should be advised that breach of a non-molestation order can be dealt with by the police as a criminal offence in the criminal court. The client should be made aware that the crime of breach of a non-molestation injunction has a maximum penalty of five years imprisonment. Whilst the Domestic Violence, Crime and Victims Act 2004 was put into place with a view to sending out an important message to defendants that the Government takes a very serious view of domestic violence, it is important to discuss with the client the implications of the client's partner facing the sanction of a custodial sentence and the likely consequences of this for the client and also any children of the family. In the event that there is a breach the police will charge the perpetrator and the client will be a witness in the criminal proceedings. Whilst the client could accept an undertaking instead of a non-molestation order under FLA 1996, s.42 the client should be advised that the courts will not necessarily accept an undertaking where the issue of violence is apparent on the face of the application. In those circumstances the courts must make an order and not accept an undertaking.

4.3.5 Solicitors should make clients aware of the possibility of costs orders within family proceedings. They should ensure that clients are aware that if they are publicly funded, and money or property is recovered or preserved in proceedings covered by the certificate, the statutory charge will apply to all costs incurred within any proceedings covered by the certificate, including proceedings for injunctive relief and children. Solicitors should explain that emergency public funding can be granted using devolved powers, but that the client must cooperate in the LSC's means assessment. If an emergency certificate is granted, it is important that the client understands that a contribution may be payable and he or she will be liable for all the costs incurred (including the difference between funded and private client rates) if the certificate is revoked (for example, for non-cooperation in the means assessment, because an offer is not accepted, or because it transpires that the client is not financially eligible without paying a contribution).

With or without notice?

4.3.6   If injunctive relief is appropriate, solicitors should discuss with clients whether it is appropriate to make a without notice application. The issues to consider are:

- whether the client may be in danger if proceedings are issued on notice;
- the seriousness of any threat to the client, including whether it is urgent and imminent;
- the likelihood of the court granting a without notice order;
- the concerns of the court with regard to the draconian nature of orders made without notice; and
- whether the client is likely to be deterred from pursuing a remedy if unable to obtain the protection of the court before the application is served upon his or her opponent.

4.3.7   If clients have taken some time to seek help about a violent incident, particularly careful consideration will need to be given as to whether it is appropriate to apply for a without notice order. The seriousness of a threat should not be dismissed simply because of delay, as any delay may not indicate the level of fear which clients may feel. Many victims of domestic abuse take some time to report the abuse. However, where possible, solicitors should make a clear legal judgment about whether courts are likely to grant a without notice order and advise in the particular circumstances. Solicitors advising or acting for publicly funded clients must have regard to the LSC's Funding Code and its decision-making guidance.

4.3.8   Solicitors should bear in mind that occupation orders are rarely granted without notice, unless the respondent is out of occupation already. Solicitors should be mindful of the court's powers to abridge service of any application from the usual two clear days to a matter of hours.

4.3.9   Solicitors should be aware of the need to have a complete note of hearing details available on request for any party who has not been present at the hearing (*W v. H (Family Division: Without Notice Orders)* [2000] 2 FLR

927). Applicants' legal representatives should also ensure that the order as drawn contains a list of all affidavits, witness statements and other evidential material read by the judge.

Length of order

4.3.10   Solicitors must give careful consideration to the proper duration of any order or power of arrest to ensure that clients have protection over a reasonable period of time. For example, courts should not limit the duration of a non-molestation order only because a power of arrest is linked to that order (see *Re B-J (A Child) (Non-Molestation Order: Power of Arrest)* [2000] 2 FCR 599).

Powers of arrest

4.3.11   The need for a power of arrest to be attached to an occupation order must be carefully considered. The practical effect of attaching a power of arrest to an order and how such orders can be enforced must be explained to clients. Clients should be advised that non-molestation orders made under FLA 1996, s.42 will have a modified penal notice endorsed drawing attention to the consequences of breach but will not carry a specific power of arrest. If the client wishes a breach of a non-molestation order to be dealt with in the civil court an application can be made for a warrant of arrest. On an on notice application for an occupation order where a respondent has used or threatened violence against an applicant or a relevant child, the court must attach a power of arrest to the order unless satisfied that they will be adequately protected without one. On a without notice application courts have the discretion to attach a power of arrest in the above circumstances, based on whether there is a risk of significant harm.

4.3.12   Where a power of arrest is attached to an occupation order and in all cases of non-molestation orders, after the order has been served on the respondent, the local police must be notified and a copy of the order delivered to them. Ideally, process servers should lodge the copy injunction order with the police immediately following service on the respondent. A receipt from the police station should be obtained whenever possible and kept on file.

4.3.13   Even where a power of arrest is not attached to an order, if there are concerns about the safety of clients, the local police's domestic violence unit should be notified in case a serious incident should arise. Solicitors must warn clients not to encourage breach of an order and of the result of doing so.

Ancillary matters

4.3.14   Where an occupation order is made under FLA 1996, consideration should be given to requesting that the court exercise its powers under FLA 1996, s.53 and Sched.7 to transfer tenancies between parties, and under s.40 to make orders concerning payment of outgoings relating to the home.

Service of orders

4.3.15   Clients must be made aware that they have a responsibility to cooperate with solicitors, enquiry agents and the police so that service of orders can be effected on respondents. If clients do not cooperate, solicitors should advise them that public funding may be withdrawn as a result.

4.3.16   Solicitors are reminded that orders should be served on respondents. It is sufficient for the respondent to be informed of the terms of the order (either by being present when the order was made or by telephone or otherwise), however, service of the order is desirable. Service of orders on respondents must be in person unless the court directs otherwise.

4.3.17   Solicitors should ensure that their client is notified when service is due to be effected and when it has been effected and discuss safety options/safety planning with them.

Criminal evidence

4.3.18   Where alleged perpetrators of domestic abuse have criminal records or there are concurrent criminal proceedings, solicitors should, where possible, introduce findings from these proceedings into the family proceedings in appropriate cases. For further information see the Law Society's book, *Related Family and Criminal Proceedings* (2007).

4.4   ACTING FOR THE RESPONDENT

Public funding

4.4.1   Solicitors should provide the following information to any clients who are respondents in proceedings for injunctions.

1.   Respondents are unlikely to qualify for a grant of legal representation unless:

   (a)   an application has been made for an occupation order (unless the respondent is already out of occupation of the property, has no good reason to return and any other issues in the proceedings are insufficient to justify public funding being used); and/or

(b) there are very serious allegations which are denied wholly or substantially; and/or

(c) there is any question of inability to defend (for example because of mental incapacity or minority).

2. Respondents in appropriate cases can be assisted and advised under Help at Court legal aid about giving undertakings.

Preparing for court

4.4.2 When a case is going to a court hearing, a solicitor, or a respondent if acting in person, should:

- wherever possible, prepare a statement in reply to the applicant's sworn statement in readiness for the hearing;
- consider what evidence could be obtained to support the respondent's case, including evidence from the housing department about the likelihood of either party being rehoused if an occupation order is made;
- consider the need for cross-applications for non-molestation and occupation orders, if there are allegations of assault on both sides.

4.4.3 If a return date is fixed, the respondent's sworn statement in reply should be filed and served as soon as possible prior to the return date. If possible, any additional evidence should be adduced before the return date. If this is not possible, the applicant's solicitors should be advised in writing of the intention to adduce further evidence, and if necessary leave should be sought at the return date hearing.

At court

4.4.4 Applicants and respondents should both be advised of the wisdom of remaining calm during any court proceedings.

4.4.5 Where possible, solicitors acting for respondents in an application for a non-molestation order should try to resolve the case by suggesting their clients give undertakings (or perhaps by the parties giving cross-undertakings). However, as a power of arrest will not attach to an undertaking, solicitors should advise respondents that there is a real possibility that an undertaking will not be accepted for that or another reason, so that clients are not given false hopes or false expectations.

4.5 OTHER PROCEEDINGS

4.5.1 Solicitors should consider and advise on whether proceedings need to be issued under the Children Act 1989 if there are concerns about where any child should live or in relation to contact arrangements between the child and their non-resident parent.

4.6 CONTACT

4.6.1 If either party has concerns about contact with any children, this should be raised at the first hearing. If contact is refused, directions can be made and an undertaking given to issue an application at that first hearing.

4.6.2 Solicitors must advise respondents of the importance of regaining the trust of parents with residence where contact is concerned. Solicitors should advise clients who are perpetrators of domestic abuse to contact the Respect national helpline for information and help, and also encourage their attendance at local perpetrator re-education programmes (see **Appendix B** for contact details).

4.7 AFTER THE HEARING

4.7.1 Solicitors should carefully check the content and wording of orders to ensure that they reflect exactly the terms of any orders specified by the judge.

4.7.2 Solicitors must ensure that orders are correctly served.

4.7.3 Solicitors must advise clients in writing of the order that has been made and the consequences of breaching it. A copy of the order should be sent to the client as soon as it is received from the court. Clients should be advised that a breach of the non-molestation order is now a criminal offence. This means that the police will take action under criminal law in respect of the breach, without needing the consent of the applicant to do so. In appropriate cases, solicitors should advise clients that any communications with applicants should be dealt with through solicitors because of the risk that any attempt to contact applicants by other means would probably be seen as harassment.

4.7.4 Solicitors should ensure that clients understand the meanings of orders and should advise parties not to act in such a way that would put the other party at risk of committal proceedings or breach of bail in criminal proceedings, for example by telephoning a party who is forbidden to contact them.

4.8   APPLICATIONS FOR ENFORCEMENT

Ensuring that orders are enforceable

4.8.1   The terms of the order must make it clear what the respondent can and cannot do.

4.8.2   Many occupation orders obtained under FLA 1996 are accompanied by powers of arrest. This means that in the event that respondents are in breach of a properly served order the police may arrest them if they violate that order and bring them before a judge within the appropriate time limits.

4.8.3   Breach of a non-molestation order is a criminal, arrestable offence. After arrest the respondent can be charged with breach of the order. The prosecution will be dealt with in the criminal court. Solicitors should note the position and the need to remind clients that the police can arrest and charge without a complaint from the client if someone else has reported the incident that amounts to a breach of the order and is prepared to give evidence.

4.8.4   If the police do not arrest for breach of a non-molestation order or the client does not want to involve the police or if no power of arrest is attached to an occupation order, the domestic abuse sufferer can deal with a breach of the order by way of a committal application, either by issuing a notice to show cause or by applying for a warrant of arrest.

4.8.5   This section of the Protocol sets out guidance as to best practice on enforcement proceedings, however generated.

Funding and costs

4.8.6   In all cases solicitors should consider possible actions with clients and advise on whether applications for committal are likely to be successful, the likely benefit to clients of making applications, the potential response of respondents to such applications and the likelihood of any costs orders being made.

Private funding

4.8.7   Solicitors should offer an estimate of costs to applicants before action is undertaken.

Public funding

4.8.8   Solicitors are reminded that in all cases they must consider whether clients are or remain eligible for public funding, check the scope, costs limit and availability of their clients' public funding certificates and ensure that they are covered for the work. Solicitors should also advise clients in relation to any resultant costs increase.

Burden of proof

4.8.9   The usual standard of proof for family law cases involves courts being satisfied on the balance of probability that clients are telling the truth. However, in committal applications the burden of proof is weightier and courts must be satisfied beyond reasonable doubt that a respondent has breached the order as alleged. This is because the respondent's liberty is at stake.

4.9   PROCEDURE AFTER BREACH

Powers of arrest

Where powers of arrest have been activated

4.9.1   Solicitors should check that powers of arrest attached to occupation orders have been properly invoked and that respondents have been arrested for breach of a term to which a power of arrest applies. In particular, it should be noted that arrest for breach of the peace (unless involving breach of one of the relevant terms of the order) will be insufficient to invoke properly a power of arrest.

4.9.2   If acting for an applicant, solicitors should ensure that their client has been notified and will attend at court. It may be helpful to remind arresting officers that they should attend with any available statements.

4.9.3   If time permits, it is helpful to provide a short statement of a client's case for the court.

4.9.4   Solicitors should consider whether it is appropriate to draft a notice to show cause to bring to the court's attention any breaches not covered by the power of arrest.

Where powers of arrest have not been activated or are not attached to the order

4.9.5   Prior to issuing an application for committal, solicitors should check that the order breached carries a penal notice which has not expired. They should discuss with clients the acts which have given rise to the allegations of breaches of orders.

4.9.6   Solicitors must explain to clients the powers of an injunction and also the limitations of court orders. Clients must be aware that some individuals will breach court orders and that they must at all times put their own and their children's safety first.

4.9.7   If breaches of court orders are reported to solicitors by applicants in injunction proceedings, the solicitor should discuss with their clients what action the clients wish to take. They should encourage clients at all times to keep records of any alleged breaches in the same way they did before the order was granted.

4.9.8   In cases where there are minor children, clients should consider the implications of the breach on any arrangements for the children including contact.

Warrants of arrest

4.9.9   Solicitors are reminded that if a power of arrest has not been attached to all or part of an order they can apply in appropriate circumstances for a warrant of arrest under FLA 1996, s.47(8). The application should be supported by evidence setting out details of the alleged breaches. Consideration should be given to how warrants will be served: practice appears to vary from area to area, but on request by the court the police may assist.

4.9.10   The use of warrants does not appear to be widespread. Practitioners should note that warrants of arrest cannot be obtained to enforce sections of an order in respect of which the police have declined to exercise a power of arrest.

Service of notice to show cause

4.9.11   Solicitors are reminded that personal service of notices to show cause is necessary and must be effected at least two days prior to the hearing, unless leave to abridge time is given. If a respondent can be shown to be avoiding service deliberately, solicitors are reminded that they will need to make an application to the court to apply for leave to serve in an alternative manner.

Open court

4.9.12 Family hearings usually take place in chambers, either in the room of the district judge or in the main court. Family clients are therefore unused to the appearance of judges and advocates in 'open court'. Clients should be advised of the difference between the chambers hearings which they will have experienced previously when obtaining orders and a committal hearing in open court, with its more formal rules of conduct.

4.9.13 Although solicitors are well used to the rules of behaviour which provide how parties should behave, clients will often be unaware of these and should be advised of court etiquette.

4.9.14 If clients wish to discuss particulars of evidence being given they should be asked to pass a note to their solicitors, or solicitors may wish to ask clients, before commencing cross examination, if any matters have arisen on which they wish their advocate to consider asking questions. Clients should be provided with paper so that they can write down these concerns.

Court proceedings

4.9.15 Solicitors should be aware of the safety implications for their clients (and potentially themselves) before, during and after hearings.

4.9.16 Solicitors acting for applicants may have to deal with respondents acting in person. Solicitors should be cautious, keep full attendance notes, and if possible ensure the presence of another person at all such exchanges. Solicitors should be aware of the possibility of incidents and potential breaches occurring during such exchanges about which the solicitor may have to give evidence. In any such case solicitors should, whenever practical, call the Law Society's Professional Ethics helpline immediately to obtain guidance as to whether they may continue to act for clients. Solicitors should consider whether it is appropriate to contact the police if such an incident occurs.

Applying for an adjournment

4.9.17 It may be necessary for either applicants or respondents to apply for an adjournment in order to obtain further evidence or if extra court time is required.

4.9.18 Solicitors should consider how best to protect the safety of applicants in the event of an adjournment, by strengthening original injunctions or by imposing bail conditions or otherwise.

4.9.19   If acting for respondents, solicitors are reminded that they may need to apply for bail.

4.9.20   Solicitors are reminded that bail conditions can be made, but not enforced, by the county court.

After the hearing

4.9.21   Whether acting for the applicant or the respondent, solicitors should explain carefully to their clients the terms of any order made and their effect. Solicitors should keep full attendance notes confirming this.

4.9.22   Solicitors should advise applicants that any further breaches should be noted and reported to the police and to them. Solicitors are reminded of the need to explain the implications of any reconciliation to clients and the need to return to court to discharge orders.

4.9.23   Solicitors must advise clients of the process of and the timescale for purging contempt of court. Solicitors should also ensure that any orders made by the court are personally served upon respondents or that the court makes an order that service be dispensed with if the respondent is in court personally.

Other issues for the respondent

4.9.24   After any injunction orders have been served, respondents should be advised of the possibility of criminal proceedings or applications for committal in the event that orders are breached. Solicitors should explain to clients the meaning of orders and how breaches might occur. They must be warned of the consequences of a breach. They should be advised that even if the applicant invites them to return to their home or contacts them in any way, respondents must refuse to communicate with applicants unless any orders prohibiting such communication have been discharged.

4.9.25   In the event that an application for committal is made, or that solicitors acting for respondents receive a letter relating to an alleged breach, clients should be advised immediately. Respondent clients should be asked to give their version of events. In the event that a breach has occurred, respondents should be advised that it is vital that they apologise when necessary. If respondents deny any or all of the breaches, this denial should be put in writing.

4.9.26   In the event that an apology is given but this does not avert a potential committal, respondent clients should be advised that they should make a statement to the court regarding their conduct. That statement should explain any reasons for an alleged breach, any mitigation, extenuating circumstances or reasons for the breach (e.g. answering a telephone call made by the applicant when the respondent has been ordered not to contact him or her).

4.9.27 In the event that the respondent has been arrested, whether under a power of arrest or otherwise, they should be seen as soon as possible, either in the police station or at court and asked to provide full details of the incident which led to the arrest. If an affidavit can be prepared at this stage it would be of assistance to the court.

4.9.28 If preparation of an affidavit is not possible, solicitors should ensure that they have taken sufficient note of the evidence to be able to give a chronological history of events and provide details of the allegations made and any response to them.

4.9.29 It may be necessary to apply for an adjournment to ensure that evidence is properly considered and the respondent's case fully put.

4.9.30 It is necessary to consider the papers served, both notices of application to show cause and statements on oath, to ensure that these comply in every respect with the statutory requirements and are not defective. (For example, orders and breaches must be particularised in notices.)

4.9.31 Respondents should be warned after any committal hearings of the possibility of further applications. In the event that a suspended committal sentence has been imposed, solicitors should ensure that respondents know what this means and the likely effect of breach.

PART 5

Children: private law

Solicitors should keep under review at all times the availability of public funding and the need to provide clients with costs information at the outset and on a regular basis.

5.1   SCOPE

5.1.1   This section applies to all private law cases involving children, with the exception of cases relating to adoption, whether these cases are brought under the Children Act 1989 or otherwise. Some of the matters contained within this Protocol are to be found within the Family Proceedings Rules (FPR) 1991, SI 1991/1247 and the Family Proceedings Courts (Children Act 1989) Rules (FPCR) 1991, SI 1991/1395 and their inclusion within the Protocol is for reinforcement in view of their importance.

5.1.2   In public law children cases solicitors are referred to **Part 6** and the Law Society's *Good Practice in Child Care Cases* (2nd edn, 2010) for guidance on appropriate methods of practice.

5.2   PARENTAL RESPONSIBILITY

5.2.1   Many biological fathers believe that they have parental responsibility when they do not. Solicitors must ensure clients are aware that a biological father only has parental responsibility if:

- he was married to the mother at the time of conception or subsequently;
- he acquired it by making a formal agreement with the mother; on the prescribed form, witnessed in the prescribed manner, which has been registered at the Principal Registry;
- in relation to a child who was registered or re-registered after 30 November 2003, he was named as the father on the child's birth certificate;

- he has been granted it by court order under the Children Act 1989, s.4 or as a consequence of being granted a residence order.

5.2.2   When instructed in any case involving a child and in which the parents are unmarried, solicitors should enquire whether the child's father has parental responsibility. When acting for a father who is not married to the mother of his child or children, solicitors who are told that the father does not have parental responsibility should advise their client about the importance of parental responsibility and consider whether or not the mother should be asked to enter into a parental responsibility agreement, or if she does not agree, whether to apply for a Children Act 1989, s.4 order.

5.2.3   When acting for one or other partner in a same sex relationship which has broken down and the future caring arrangements for a child or children arises, care should be taken to advise on the issue of parental responsibility and how this might be acquired by the making of an agreement, residence order or, in appropriate cases, a joint residence order.

5.3   PROTECTIVE MEASURES AND CONFIDENTIALITY

5.3.1   In cases concerning allegations of domestic abuse and child abuse, whether physical, sexual or emotional, solicitors should, wherever possible, encourage clients to inform the appropriate authority. Solicitors should consider this paragraph in conjunction with **5.3.6**.

5.3.2   Solicitors should have up-to-date details of all relevant local support agencies, such at the Women's Centre, local Refuge accommodation agencies and counselling services and be able to signpost clients to any agencies which may be of assistance to them or their children, as a matter of urgency.

5.3.3   The courts must now give proper consideration to the impact on children witnessing (whether by seeing or hearing) domestic abuse against a parent (see *Re L, V, M and H* [2000] 2 FLR 334). Clients should not be pressed into agreeing contact in circumstances where they genuinely believe it is not in the interests of the children to see the absent parent or where they believe that the absent parent may be using the proceedings to continue their harassment. The court has a duty to conduct a fact-finding hearing in full when domestic violence is alleged (*Re Z (Children) (Unsupervised contact; allegations of domestic violence)* [2009] 3 FCR 80).

5.3.4   The effect on children of seeing someone being subjected to domestic abuse, or of being directly abused either physically, sexually or emotionally by the perpetrator during contact, or of being alone with the perpetrator of violence should not be underestimated (see the report to the Lord Chancellor prepared by the Advisory Board on Family Law Children Act Sub-Committee (CASC) in March 2000: *Guidelines for Good Practice on Parental Contact in Cases where there is Domestic Violence* (available as archived material at **www.dca.gov.uk**)). Solicitors should be fully familiar with the *Practice Direction (Residence and Contact Orders – Domestic Violence and Harm (No.2))* [2009] 2 FLR 1400 (as amended in the light of *Re B (Care Proceedings; Standard of proof)* [2008] 2 FLR 14 (see **Appendix A**). Advice should be realistic but sufficiently robust to support clients should their individual circumstances raise questions about the appropriateness of contact.

5.3.5   Solicitors should be aware of the extended definition of 'harm' to children contained within the Adoption and Children Act 2002, s.120. This amends the Children Act 1989 definition of harm to include 'impairment suffered from seeing or hearing the ill-treatment of another'. Solicitors will be aware that in making or responding to an application under the Children Act 1989, s.8 made on Form C100, Form C1A is specifically designed to raise issues of domestic violence at the time of issue. This in turn will inform the safeguarding and screening work undertaken by Cafcass prior to the first hearing dispute resolution appointment (FHDRA). Solicitors should routinely screen for domestic abuse, in addition to using the forms, whether or not clients raise it as an issue.

5.3.6   Solicitors should be aware of, and in appropriate circumstances, must make clients aware of, the effect of the Solicitors' Code of Conduct 2007, rule 4, guidance note 13, which states the exceptional circumstances in which solicitors should consider revealing confidential information to an appropriate authority:

> There may be exceptional circumstances involving children where a solicitor should consider revealing confidential information to an appropriate authority. This may be where the child is the client and the child reveals information which indicates continuing sexual or other physical abuse but refuses to allow disclosure of such information. Similarly, there may be situations where an adult discloses abuse either by himself or herself or by another adult against a child but refuses to allow any disclosure. [The solicitor] must consider whether the threat to the child's life or health, both mental and physical is sufficiently serious to justify a breach of the duty of confidentiality.

Solicitors are reminded that they are obliged to disclose the whereabouts of a child who is the subject of a 'seek and locate' order or a child who is a ward of the court or otherwise if so directed by the court, regardless of the rules of client confidentiality. If solicitors feel concerned that such disclosure puts a client and/or their child or children at risk they must seek directions from the court as a matter of urgency.

5.3.7   However, solicitors should always bear in mind that they owe a duty of confidentiality to their clients and may have to justify any breach of that duty to their professional body. It is always advisable to seek advice from the Law Society's Professional Ethics department (see **Appendix B** for contact details), other members of the profession, partners in the firm and professional insurers.

5.3.8   In cases where an applicant does not know the address of the respondent and the respondent has care of the relevant child or children, solicitors should consider seeking a direction from the court for disclosure of the respondent's address to the court by the appropriate government agency. This may be more economical than obtaining a 'seek and locate' order.

5.4   ABDUCTION

5.4.1   Solicitors must recognise that child abduction law is a rapidly developing and highly specialist area of law and that specialist advice is absolutely essential for clients. Please refer to **Part 7** for more detailed information on child abduction matters.

5.5   CHILD CONTACT CENTRES

5.5.1   Child contact centres are a valuable (although limited) resource and solicitors should be aware of their local centres and the facilities and services which they provide. Child contact centres have agreed to adhere to national standards. The *Revised Protocol for Referrals of Families by Judges and Magistrates to Child Contact Centres* (2010) has been developed by the National Association of Child Contact Centres (NACCC) and endorsed by leading members of the judiciary (see **www.naccc.org.uk**).

5.5.2   The majority of child contact centres provide supported contact whereby contact can take place in the centre or children can be handed from one parent to the other. Consideration should also be given to the appropriateness of arranging a handover using third parties and keeping parents apart with no face-to-face contact with each other. Solicitors should explain to clients the difference between supported and supervised contact before the first contact visit at a centre occurs.

5.5.3   Where violence is an issue, careful thought should be given to the use of child contact centres. In cases when domestic violence is alleged (especially where there have been criminal proceedings or injunctive relief), supervised contact may well be necessary, at least initially, pending any fact-finding hearing involving serious allegations of violence or other abuse. Solicitors should also be alive to the fact that violence can take place outside the contact centre, when parties are arriving or leaving. There are a small number of child contact centres which undertake high vigilance supervision and the NACCC has details of its member centres which provide this service (see **Appendix B** for contact details). It is often useful for clients to visit the child contact centre before the first contact period takes place.

5.5.4   Child contact centres are not equipped to deal with abusers who pose a serious threat to their families and it is vital that the centre coordinator is given the full background (orally, if necessary) in order to decide whether the centre can accommodate the family. Referral forms must be completed as fully and accurately as possible. It is important that child contact centres have full information about details of violent or abusive behaviour.

5.5.5   Solicitors must make it clear on referral forms if they are requesting that other family members can be present during the contact visit. Solicitors for the resident parent should discuss with them the need to prepare the child for the visit.

5.5.6   Solicitors have a duty of confidentiality to their clients and cannot reveal details about their client without the client's consent. If clients refuse to give consent to reveal information required on the referral form, a referral should not be made.

5.5.7   No child contact centre can guarantee that a child will not be removed from it. It is vital that centres are warned if there is a fear of this or if there have been threats of abduction. If so, solicitors should discuss with the resident parent the feasibility of giving the centre recent photographs of the children and of the contact parent. If there is a possibility of abduction abroad, solicitors for parents with residence should be asked to retain the passports of parents having contact and/or those of the children to ensure safe contact can take place. An application to court for appropriate orders should also be considered.

5.5.8   If it is not possible to access an appropriate contact service, the issue of face-to-face contact should be carefully reviewed. Other forms of contact may be appropriate such as e-mails, webcam and telephone calls. Contact via social networking sites may be attractive to clients but presents the potential for abuse and interference by third parties and is generally not favoured by the courts. In serious cases, consideration should be given to whether it is appropriate to seek an order for no contact.

5.5.9   Solicitors should advise their clients that they should inform contact centres when they no longer need to use them. Clients should be made aware that child contact centres are regarded by the court as a temporary solution to difficulties in contact and not a permanent arrangement.

5.5.10   Solicitors should make clients aware that, in general, volunteers and staff at child contact centres do not provide reports or statements for any type of court proceedings unless a child is believed to be at risk of harm. However, a few supervised child contact centres are an exception to this general rule.

5.6   MEDIATION AND COLLABORATIVE LAW

5.6.1   Solicitors should recognise that alternative methods of dispute resolution, such as mediation and collaborative law, can be particularly helpful in dealing with disputes over contact and residence. However, solicitors must bear in mind that this may be neither a safe nor suitable option in domestic abuse cases. Mediators do carry out their own screening to identify issues such as domestic violence and power imbalance between parents or carers.

5.6.2   It is recognised that the availability of mediation and alternative dispute resolution (ADR) varies across the country. Mediators offering both publicly funded and privately funded family mediation are available across England and Wales. Mediators are able to offer mediation for disputes over issues regarding children (including contact and residence). Only those mediators with a franchise can offer mediation which will be funded by the LSC. Solicitors acting for publicly funded clients must ensure that they have the correct level of public funding in place for their clients at all stages of the mediation and legal process.

5.6.3   Where out of court mediation is readily available, solicitors must consider referring clients to such mediation before issuing an application at the court. In publicly funded cases, this is a prerequisite to moving from Family Help (Lower) to Family Help (Higher) for the purpose of bringing court proceedings, except in certain closely defined circumstances. Solicitors should always be aware of the availability of mediation and ADR once proceedings have been issued. Some courts do arrange for mediators to be present at the FHDRA. Even if this resource is not available, Cafcass or the court itself may reccommend a referral to an independent mediation service at this stage in proceedings or at some later stage. In this context solicitors should be fully familiar with Parenting Information Programme (PIP) arrangements in their local court area as courts are increasingly making orders referring parents to these. Participation is designed to enable separated parents to acquire more understanding of the impact of parental conflict and negative words and behaviour on children and encourages and promotes positive co-parenting. Where court-based mediation or concilia-tion schemes managed by Cafcass are only available once proceedings have been issued, it may be necessary to issue proceedings early on.

5.6.4 Solicitors must remember that some family structures and community dynamics are built on unequal power relations between the parties and that some inequalities may be legitimised by culture and religion. In these cases, solicitors and mediators should be aware that mediation may not be appropriate or seek help from specialist mediators in that culture/religion where available.

5.7   THE REVISED PRIVATE LAW PROGRAMME

5.7.1 Solicitors should be fully familiar with the Revised Private Law Pro-gramme issued as a Practice Direction by the President of the Family Division and effective from 1 April 2010 (*Practice Direction (Revised Private Law Programme)* [2010] 2 FLR 717). It is designed to provide a framework for the consistent national approach to the resolution of the issues in private family law whilst enabling local practices and initiatives to be operated in addition and within the framework (para.1.6).

5.7.2 Solicitors should understand how the Revised Private Law Programme affects the role of Cafcass and be aware of any local initiatives within the scheme, including in-court conciliation schemes, family resolution pilots or other resources offered locally. They must bear in mind the solicitor's role in early dispute resolution and in case management.

5.8   BEFORE ISSUE OF PROCEEDINGS

5.8.1 Court proceedings should normally only be commenced if all reasonable avenues have been considered and found to be inappropriate or unworkable or if this is the only way to offer the parties the opportunity of a mediated settlement.

5.8.2 Solicitors should be aware of the content of *Practice Direction (Represen-tation of Children in Family Proceedings)* [2004] 1 FLR 1188; *Practice Note (Cafcass: Representation of Children in Family Proceedings)* [2004] 1 FLR 1190 and the Cafcass guidance *Representation of Children in Private Law Proceedings* (2004) (see **Appendix A**) or any revision of the same. They must consider whether a child needs to be legally represented in any proceedings which relate to them. Solicitors should be aware of the role of Cafcass in safeguarding and identifying risk and more particularly Cafcass policy in cases involving allegations of domestic abuse.

5.8.3 Solicitors should be aware of any facilities in their local family proceedings and county courts including:

- provision of separate waiting areas and other facilities for parties;
- facilities for children including playrooms, etc;
- availability of in-court Cafcass conciliation facilities;
- facilities for vulnerable parties and witnesses both in court and whilst waiting to be called;
- waiting times for first hearings and subsequent ones through to final hearings.

5.8.4 Solicitors may wish to direct clients to the Cafcass website (see **www.cafcass.co.uk**) and refer them to the age appropriate leaflets which Cafcass produces for children, which explain the role of Cafcass officers within proceedings. Age appropriate information is also available from other organisations such as Childline (see **Appendix B**). Solicitors should be aware of and keep available leaflets for children and parents affected by relationship breakdown which can be obtained via the local Court Centre or from the Ministry of Justice. These are designed to help children in different age groups to understand the changes that are occurring and to assist parents in discussing matters with them.

5.9 ISSUE OF PROCEEDINGS AND THEREAFTER

5.9.1 Forms C100 (and C1A if appropriate) or other documents should be simply worded using factual, rather than emotive language, setting out clearly the order sought. Solicitors may find it helpful to append a parenting plan indicating the proposed arrangements for the children.

5.9.2 Form C1A includes an opportunity briefly to identify issues of domestic abuse which may be relevant to the application. Solicitors should assist their clients to complete the form as accurately and unemotionally as possible and should remember that the application form should not be used as a statement of evidence.

5.9.3 No evidence should be filed until ordered by the court as stated in FPCR 1991, although it is good practice to prepare a short statement in readiness for an ex parte interim hearing if relevant.

5.9.4 Solicitors should avoid drafting statements using emotive and/or inflammatory language and/or expressing subjective opinions. They should ensure that statements drafted reflect as closely as possible the client's instructions and language, particularly when there are language difficulties. Where English is not the client's first language, solicitors should always consider whether an interpreter should be present throughout an interview. Solicitors must consider whether they can properly act for a client when they do not speak the language of the client and no interpreter is available.

5.9.5   Solicitors should at all times be mindful of the impact of domestic abuse upon children. The Adoption and Children Act 2002, s.120 amends the Children Act 1989 definition of harm to include 'impairment suffered from seeing or hearing the ill-treatment of another'. Solicitors should advise their clients that children who have heard or witnessed domestic abuse are taken to fall within the amended definition of children who have suffered harm. Clients should be advised that as part of the safeguarding and screening work undertaken by Cafcass prior to the FHDRA this issue will be addressed and Cafcass is likely to recommend to the court that there should be a fact-finding hearing if the allegations of domestic violence are not accepted by the parent or parents against whom they are alleged.

5.9.6   Where alleged perpetrators of domestic abuse have criminal records or there are concurrent criminal proceedings, solicitors should introduce findings from these proceedings into the family proceedings where relevant.

5.9.7   Solicitors should be aware of the potential effects of the Domestic Violence, Crime and Victims Act 2004 in children cases.

5.9.8   Clients must be advised that a court will have regard, inter alia, to the ascertainable wishes and feelings of the child concerned, considered in light of that child's age and understanding, and to other matters as set out in the welfare test at Children Act 1989, s.1.

5.9.9   Solicitors must advise their clients about the need for confidentiality in proceedings relating to children and the fact that documents produced for proceedings relating to children, particularly the report of the Children and Family Reporter (Cafcass officer), may not be disclosed to those who are not parties to the proceedings without permission of the court (FPR 1991, rule 4.23 and FPCR 1991, rule 23). Solicitors must be aware of the impact that the Children Act 2004, s.62 and revisions to FPR 1991 have on disclosure.

5.9.10   Solicitors should be familiar with the Practice Direction issued by the President of the Family Division on 20 April 2009 dealing with attendance of media representatives at hearings of family proceedings in the High Court, county court and Family Proceedings Court (see **Appendix A**). The Practice Direction applying to the High Court and county court supplements FPR 1991, rule 10.28 and the Practice Direction applying to the

Family Proceedings Court supplements FPCR 1991, rule 16A. In broad terms, they deal with the right that the media have to attend such hearings subject to the discretion of the court to exclude them.

5.9.11 Solicitors should advise clients on the need (if any) for witnesses. Solicitors should consider carefully the need to adduce evidence from non-parties, and should guard against a proliferation of witnesses who may add nothing to the case and may be pursuing an agenda unrelated to the welfare of the child. Solicitors are referred generally to *Practice Direction (Family Proceedings: Case Management)* [1995] 1 FLR 456, para.3.7.3).

5.9.12 Solicitors should advise clients that it will not assist them to produce statements or letters written by their children, nor to bring their children to speak with solicitors acting for one or other parent, and solicitors should firmly discourage such conduct. Solicitors should not see the children who are the subject of any case in which they are advising unless they are acting for the child.

5.9.13 Solicitors should encourage clients to remember that in most cases they will be continuing to co-parent with the other party and it is better to acknowledge the other party's strengths as a parent rather than to condemn his or her weaknesses in an inflammatory or negative statement. This approach may not, however, be appropriate in cases involving domestic violence or dealing with a parent exhibiting an aggressive, controlling or oppositional approach to the case to the detriment of the child or children's welfare.

5.9.14 The court will wish to have as balanced a view as possible. If clients insist on the inclusion of subjective opinions in their statements, for example, as to the other party's adviser, solicitors should consider whether guidance should be sought from the Law Society's Professional Ethics department (for contact details, see **Appendix B**) and in any event whether they should continue to act.

5.9.15 Solicitors should be aware that they have a duty to the LSC to ensure that public funds are not utilised unreasonably. If a client is insisting on a course of action that is unreasonable, the solicitor is under a duty to inform the LSC of this.

Court reports

5.9.16 Clients should be advised of the role of the Children and Family Reporter (Cafcass officer) or local authority social worker in the decision-making and information-gathering process when they are asked to assist by the court. They should be made aware of the importance of the officer's report and should be encouraged to cooperate with the reporter and advised that failure to do so could prejudice their case. Clients should be advised that the work of the Cafcass officer includes ensuring that the wishes and feelings of the children are conveyed to the court.

5.9.17 Over the past two years, and more particularly following the introduction of the Revised Private Law Programme, the role of the Cafcass officer is now more clearly defined and courts are required to consider carefully in all cases whether a report is necessary and if one is required to identify specifically the issue or issues to be addressed. Solicitors should advise clients that they may be required to contribute to the cost of obtaining such a report.

5.9.18 Solicitors should be aware of, and where appropriate advise clients on, the right of a child to apply to be joined as a party to the proceedings in the event that the Children and Family Reporter (Cafcass officer) makes this recommendation or the court is otherwise persuaded that it is appropriate to make a direction to this effect under FPR 1991, rule 9.5. Solicitors are referred to *Practice Direction (Representation of Children in Family Proceedings)* [2004] 1 FLR 1188, particularly para.3.

5.9.19 Where English is not the client's first language, solicitors are referred to the advice on interpreters given at **5.9.4**.

Experts

5.9.20 The President of the Family Division issued a very comprehensive Practice Direction dealing with the use of expert evidence and the instructing of experts in Family Proceedings relating to children, which came into force on 1 April 2008 (see **Appendix A**). It is a very comprehensive guide dealing with the instructing of experts, duties of experts, the content of their reports, expert meetings and the calling of experts to give evidence. The Annex to the Practice Direction even suggests specimen questions to be put depending on the expertise involved. The Practice Direction is an invaluable and crucial document and should always be referred to when instructing an expert.

5.9.21 When selecting an expert recent and relevant experience is essential. An up-to-date CV should be sought from the proposed expert.

5.9.22 Experts should only be instructed and indeed their evidence will only be admitted where necessary, that is in cases where other available evidence does not deal with the relevant issue and where the welfare of the child dictates that such further evidence ought to be obtained.

5.9.23 Solicitors must advise clients that they must not take children to appointed experts, nor obtain experts' reports, without prior permission from the court.

5.9.24 Parties should be encouraged to use a single expert jointly instructed if this is appropriate in the circumstances of the case. The costs of such an expert should be apportioned between the parties whenever possible. When clients are publicly funded, solicitors must report to the LSC if clients will not agree to the use of a single expert where that would be appropriate to the case. The joint instruction of experts should be encouraged in appropriate cases. In some instances, however, unrepresented parties or those not eligible for public funding will not be expected to bear the cost of the expert, this cost being borne by publicly funded parties. The letter of instruction will fall to one of the parties to prepare and its contents should be agreed (if possible) by the other parties. The letter of instruction, whether agreed or not, is discloseable.

5.9.25 Solicitors need to be aware of the provisions of the Solicitors' Code of Conduct 2007, rule 4 (guidance note 14) and their duty to disclose experts' reports in proceedings under the Children Act 1989. The full text of note 14 is reproduced below.

> 14. In proceedings under the Children Act 1989 you are under a duty to reveal experts' reports commissioned for the purposes of proceedings, as these reports are not privileged. The position in relation to voluntary disclosure of other documents or solicitor/client communications is uncertain. Under 11.01, an advocate is under a duty not to mislead the court., Therefore, if you are an advocate, and have certain knowledge which you realise is adverse to the client's case, you may be extremely limited in what you can state in the client's favour. In this situation, you should seek the client's agreement for full voluntary disclosure for three reasons:
>
> (a)   the matters the client wants to hide will probably emerge anyway;
> (b)   you will be able to do a better job for the client if all the relevant information is presented to the court; and
> (c)   if the information is not voluntarily disclosed, you may be severely criticised by the court.
>
> If the client refuses to give you authority to disclose the relevant information, you are entitled to refuse to continue to act for the client if to do so will place you in breach of your obligations to the court.

Clients should be advised of the above.

5.9.26 Whether or not an expert is instructed jointly, the expert must be prepared to answer reasonable questions raised by any party.

Management of court proceedings

5.9.27   In the recent past, there have been a variety of court practices throughout the jurisdiction in managing private law cases. Moves towards standardisation of procedure by a Private Law Programme have resulted in the introduction of the Revised Private Law Programme by way of a Practice Direction made by the President of the Family Division, effective from 1 April 2010 (see **Appendix A**). The aims of the programme have been referred to at **5.7.1**.

5.9.28   In essence, following issue of proceedings, Cafcass will undertake safeguarding and risk identification work, incorporating that in a prescribed form (the Schedule 2 Report) which the court will have together with Form C100 (C1A if appropriate) and C7 Response and C1A if appropriate at the FHDRA. The emphasis at that hearing will be, where appropriate, to see early resolution of cases; Cafcass and, where available, a local mediation service should be in attendance to facilitate this in appropriate cases.

5.9.29   At all stages in proceedings, solicitors should inform the court listing section as soon as it becomes clear that a case's time estimate has changed and provide a revised time estimate. It is desirable for both parties' solicitors to agree any such change but even if agreement cannot be reached the court should still be notified.

5.9.30   In all cases, other than those listed for one hour or less or very urgent cases, solicitors should be fully familiar with the *Practice Direction (Family Proceedings: Court Bundles) (Universal Practice to be applied in all Courts other than the Family Proceedings Court)* [2006] 2 FLR 199 (see **Appendix A**). Failure to comply can result in the making of a wasted costs order.

5.9.31   Whenever possible, solicitors should try to agree in advance with other parties those parts of the evidence which are agreed and advise the court of agreed facts to allow the court to focus on areas remaining in dispute.

5.9.32   Solicitors must, where necessary, obtain an appropriate direction of the court to ensure the attendance of the Cafcass officer, as provided in FPR 1991, and must never assume the author of a report prepared for the court by either Cafcass or a social worker will attend unless directed to do so.

5.9.33   Solicitors must be aware, and make their clients aware, that they will need to exercise restraint when questioning a Children and Family Reporter, although cross-examination of Cafcass officers is now provided for in FPR 1991.

5.10 AFTER THE CONCLUSION OF PROCEEDINGS

5.10.1 Solicitors must write to clients confirming the outcome of proceedings and returning, where available, any original documents which clients have provided.

5.10.2 Solicitors must remind clients of the confidential nature of the proceedings and any relevant documents.

5.10.3 Solicitors should advise clients of the mechanism for review of decisions and, unless clearly inappropriate, remind them of the possibility of mediation as a means of resolving future disputes.

5.10.4 Where solicitors have given an undertaking in relation, for example, to safekeeping of documents, they should remember to seek to have the undertaking discharged at the conclusion of proceedings.

5.10.5 Solicitors should consider with their clients (and perhaps with the Cafcass officer) how the child is to be told the results of proceedings, particularly when the child has expressed views which have not been accepted by the court. When a child is separately represented pursuant to FPR 1991, rule 9.5 this will be done by the children's guardian in connection with and in consultation with the solicitor for the child.

5.11 CHILD SUPPORT ISSUES

5.11.1 Please refer to **Part 8** for more detailed information on child support.

Child interveners in ancillary relief

5.11.2 A child may intervene in proceedings to his parents' divorce if the child has, or appears to have, an interest in the matrimonial assets. In such cases the child should be represented by a guardian ad litem (FPR 1991, rule 9.2). There will seldom be a suitable family member and an application should be made for the appointment of the Official Solicitor, subject to his consent, to represent the minor or minors in the proceedings. FPR 1991, rule 9.2A does not apply to proceedings under the Domicile and Matrimonial Proceedings Act 1973.

5.12 ADOPTION AND SURROGACY

5.12.1 Adoption is included in the parallel Law Society publication *Good Practice in Child Care Cases* (2nd edn, 2010) as most domestic adoption proceedings follow on from public law proceedings and the making of care and placement orders in respect of a child in care, or where a child has been relinquished by birth parents into care with a view to adoption.

5.12.2   However, there are some domestic adoption cases which do not relate to children in the care system or public law proceedings. Such cases include private adoption placements within the close family, which are still lawful under the Adoption and Children Act (ACA) 2002. There may also be cases which contravene ACA 2002, s.92 as private placements where prospective adopters are not close relatives of the birth parents within the definition of 'relatives'. These proceedings are likely to be transferred to High Court level.

5.12.3   Step-parent adoptions also fall into the category of private adoption. An application for a step-parent adoption order can now be made by the step-parent alone (ACA 2002, s.51(2)) rather than as previously, having to be made by the biological parent and the step-parent together. However, when advising a step-parent who wishes to adopt, other options for the step-parent to obtain parental responsibility should be considered, such as entering into a step-parent agreement or applying for a step-parent order under ACA 2002, s.112(1), or a residence order.

5.12.4   Surrogacy as an option for parenthood is gaining increasing significance. Parental orders under the Human Fertilisation and Embryology Act (HFEA) 2008, recognising commissioning couples in surrogacy arrangements as the sole parents of the child, have been extended to include unmarried couples, both heterosexual and same sex in enduring family relationships, and civil partners, in addition to the existing recognition of married couples (HFEA 2008, s.54(2)).

5.12.5   International adoption and surrogacy are also becoming more significant areas of practice. In both, the interface between adoption or surrogacy law and immigration law must be considered and it will frequently be necessary to advise clients who are considering either to seek parallel immigration advice.

5.12.6   International adoptions can be recognised in this country if the country from which a British family is adopting has either ratified the Hague Convention on Protection of Children and Co-operation in Respect of Intercountry Adoption 1993 (the Hague Convention) or is listed on the Adoption (Designation of Overseas Adoptions) Order 1973, SI 1973/19 (the Designated List). If the child's country is neither a Hague Convention nor a Designated List country then the only other way the foreign adoption can be recognised here and the child acquire British nationality is by an adoption order being made in the British courts.

5.12.7   International surrogacy involves complex questions of immigration and children's law and will normally require clients considering parenthood by this method to seek such advice both in this country and in the country where the surrogacy arrangement is being made.

5.12.8   In all surrogacy cases whether domestic or international, solicitors should take care not to contravene the law in respect of commercial surrogacy in the Surrogacy Arrangements Act 1985, by facilitating or being involved in negotiating a surrogacy arrangement on behalf of a client.

PART 6

Children: public law

6.1 GENERAL

6.1.1 Solicitors should follow the *Good Practice Guide in Child Care Cases*, (2nd edn, Law Society, 2010).

6.1.2 In particular, solicitors should have regard to the general principles and common issues in the Guide – most notably:

- child focus – the child's interests are paramount;
- a non-adversarial approach;
- courtesy and professionalism in all dealings with other parties;
- testing the evidence;
- a professional approach;
- case management;
- avoiding delay;
- awareness of human rights and diversity issues.

6.2 KEY CONCEPTS

6.2.1 These are set out in the Children Act (CA) 1989.

The welfare test

6.2.2 See CA 1989, s.1(1):

(1) When a court determines any question with respect to—

(a) the upbringing of a child; or
(b) the administration of a child's property or the application of any income arising from it,

the child's welfare shall be the court's paramount consideration.

The welfare checklist

6.2.3   See CA 1989, s.1(3) and (4):

    (3)   In the circumstances mentioned in subsection (4), a court shall have regard in particular to –

        (a)   the ascertainable wishes and feelings of the child concerned (considered in the light of his age and understanding);

        (b)   his physical, emotional and educational needs;

        (c)   the likely effect on him of any change in his circumstances;

        (d)   his age, sex, background and any characteristics of his which the court considers relevant;

        (e)   any harm which he has suffered or is at risk of suffering;

        (f)   how capable each of his parents, and any other person in relation to whom the court considers the question to be relevant, is of meeting his needs;

        (g)   the range of powers available to the court under this Act in the proceedings in question.

    (4)   The circumstances are that –

        (a)   the court is considering whether to make, vary or discharge a section 8 order, and the making, variation or discharge of the order is opposed by any party to the proceedings; or

        (b)   the court is considering whether to make, vary or discharge a special guardianship order or an order under Part IV.

Delay

6.2.4   In any proceedings in which any question with respect to the upbringing of a child arises, the court shall have regard to the general principle that any delay in determining the question is likely to prejudice the welfare of the child (CA 1989, s.1(2)).

'No order' principle

6.2.5   Where a court is considering whether or not to make one or more orders under CA 1989 with respect to a child, it shall not make the order or any of the orders unless it considers that doing so would be better for the child than making no order at all (CA 1989, s.1(5)).

Parental responsibility

6.2.6   In CA 1989, s.3, 'parental responsibility' means all the rights, duties, powers, responsibilities and authority which by law a parent of a child has in relation to the child and his property.

6.2.7   Solicitors should be clear who has parental responsibility. Individuals who may have parental responsibility are set out in CA 1989 (as amended by subsequent legislation) (see **5.2**))

6.3   DUTIES OF LOCAL AUTHORITIES

6.3.1   Part III of CA 1989 sets out the duties and powers that local authorities have in relation to provision of services for children in need and their families, provision of accommodation for children and the duties owed to children who are 'looked after'.

Section 47 investigations

6.3.2   The local authority has a duty to commence a section 47 investigation where they (CA 1989, s.47(1)):

(a)   are informed that a child who lives, or is found, in their area –

(i)   is the subject of an emergency protection order; or
(ii)   is in police protection; or
(iii)   has contravened a ban imposed by a curfew notice within the meaning of Chapter I of Part I of the Crime and Disorder Act 1998; or

(b)   have reasonable cause to suspect that a child who lives, or is found, in their area is suffering, or is likely to suffer, significant harm.

If the above test is satisfied the local authority 'shall make or cause to be made, such enquiries as they consider necessary to enable it to decide whether it should take any action to safeguard or promote the child's welfare'.

6.3.3   Where the local authority has obtained an emergency protection order in relation to a child, there are additional requirements that require consideration as part of the investigation.

6.3.4   Section 53(3) of the Children Act (CA) 2004 places a new duty on the local authority when conducting an investigation under CA 1989, s.47. Section 47(5A) (as amended) holds that for the purpose of making a determination under the section as to any action to be taken in respect of a child, the local authority shall 'so far as reasonably practicable and consistent with the child's welfare' ascertain the child's wishes and feelings about the action to be taken in relation to him or her and give due consideration (having regard to the child's age and understanding) to the wishes and feelings that have been ascertained.

6.3.5   The possible outcomes of the section 47 investigation are:

- no further action is considered necessary;
- the possibility of significant harm is believed to exist but no real evidence has been found and so careful monitoring is required;
- the concerns are substantiated but it is judged that there is no subsisting risk of significant harm in which case a plan might be able to be agreed between the closest agencies involved and the family and child; or
- there is a continuing risk of harm and so a child protection conference should be initiated.

6.4   ASSESSMENTS

Initial assessments

6.4.1   Where a referral is made to the local authority about a child who may be in need, the local authority must decide within one working day of the referral whether to undertake an initial assessment. If appropriate, it should be carried out within 10 working days. It may be concluded that no further action is necessary. If further action is proposed, it can take a variety of forms.

Child protection conferences

6.4.2   A child protection conference may be called. It is made up of the key professionals involved with the family. The parents will also be invited and may be accompanied by a friend or legal representative. Children may also participate if they are of sufficient age and understanding and wish to do so.

6.4.3   If the conference is concerned that a child is at risk of significant harm, a child protection plan is drawn up to set out what is needed to safeguard and promote the welfare of the child. This is likely to involve the carrying out of a core assessment (see below). The child protection plan must be kept under review at subsequent conferences (known as child protection reviews).

6.4.4   Solicitors are referred to the statutory guidance contained in *Working Together to Safeguard Children* (Department for Education, March 2010). This guidance governs the operation of child protection conferences and child protection plans.

Core assessments

6.4.5   In all cases where an initial assessment concludes that there is cause to suspect that a child is suffering or is likely to suffer significant harm a core assessment must be completed. This should be within 35 working days. Guidance on the completion of the assessment is contained in *Working Together* and the *Framework for the Assessment of Children in Need and their Families* (Department of Health, 2000).

6.4.6   The core assessment is viewed as a key assessment tool for local authorities and should be presented to a court in the event that care proceedings become necessary.

6.5   CARE PROCEEDINGS

Pre-proceedings requirements

6.5.1   If a local authority is unable to assist a parent in removing the risk of significant harm to a child, it may need to commence care proceedings.

6.5.2   Except in cases of emergency, a local authority should not resort to care proceedings without considering alternative courses of action and following the pre-proceedings requirements set out in statutory guidance (see revised Volume 1 of the *Children Act 1989 Guidance and Regulations* ('Guidance': available through **www.education.gov.uk**).

6.5.3   The Guidance and the *Practice Direction (Public Law Proceedings) (Guide to Case Management)*, April 2010 (commonly known as the Public Law Outline) 'front load' the processes whereby local authorities may need to consider commencing care proceedings. Local authorities should work in partnership with parents to safeguard the welfare of children in need. If this is not possible and there is perceived to be a risk of significant harm to children, local authorities should consider other measures, e.g. holding a family group conference, further preventative work, identification and assessment of extended family members as potential carers (NB: CA 1989, s.17 duty to promote the upbringing of children by their families) and the accommodation of a child under CA 1989, s.20.

6.5.4   If the local authority considers that it may be necessary to institute care proceedings, it should send a 'Letter Before Proceedings' to the parents setting out the concerns for the child, what attempts have been made to date to address the concerns, what needs to be done further to address the concerns and inviting the parent to a 'pre-proceedings meeting' to discuss the issues. This is aimed at ensuring that parents have been made aware of all of the local authority concerns about the relevant child, before they reach a decision to apply for care or supervision orders. At that point, a parent or person with parental responsibility is able to access non-means/ non-merit public funding and may be accompanied to the meeting by a solicitor.

6.5.5   The procedure to be followed at pre-proceedings meetings will vary between local authorities, but solicitors should have regard to *Preparing for Care and Supervision Proceedings*, a best practice guide for use by all professionals involved with children and families pre-proceedings for applications made under CA 1989, s.31, produced by the Care Proceedings Programme, Ministry of Justice (August 2009) (see **Appendix A**). This provides valuable guidance on best practice in the pre-proceedings phase.

6.5.6   At the pre-proceedings meeting, a plan may be drawn up setting out the expectations of the parents and what the local authority will do to assist. It will then be subject to regular review at any subsequent meetings.

6.5.7   If such a plan is not possible or viewed as safe for the child, the local authority may decide to commence proceedings. Even in situations where is it not deemed appropriate to apply for an emergency protection order (EPO), it can be necessary to make an immediate s.31 application (Guidance, para.3.30).

6.5.8   The local authority may bypass these procedures in cases of emergency. Local authorities are encouraged in such circumstances to go straight to court.

6.5.9   In summary, solicitors should refer to:

- the statutory guidance as revised April 2010: *Children Act 1989, Guidance and Regulations*, volume 1 'Court orders';
- the Public Law Outline – revised version issued 2010 (see **6.5.3** and **www.hmcourts-service.gov.uk/cms/files/ public_law_outline_PD_April_2010.pdf**);
- the Ministry of Justice Care Proceedings Programme best rractice guide – *Preparing for Care and Supervision Proceedings* (August 2009).

See **Appendix A** for website links.

Going to court

Grounds for a care/supervision order

6.5.10   In order to obtain a care or supervision order, the local authority must establish that the threshold criteria are met. These are set out in CA 1989, s.31(2):

> A court may only make a care order or supervision order if it is satisfied –
>
> (a)   that the child concerned is suffering, or is likely to suffer, significant harm; and
> (b)   that the harm, or likelihood of harm, is attributable to—
>
>> (i)   the care given to the child, or likely to be given to him if the order were not made, not being what it would be reasonable to expect a parent to give to him; or
>> (ii)   the child's being beyond parental control.

6.5.11   Definitions in the CA 1989 are as follows (s.31(9)):

> 'harm' means ill-treatment or the impairment of health or development including, for example, impairment suffered from seeing or hearing the ill-treatment of another;
> 'development' means physical, intellectual, emotional, social or behavioural development;
> 'health' means physical or mental health; and
> 'ill-treatment' includes sexual abuse and forms of ill-treatment which are not physical.

6.5.12   If the court finds the threshold criteria satisfied (the threshold stage), it must then go on to consider how the case should be disposed of (the disposal stage). The court must then consider the welfare test, the welfare checklist, the 'no order' principle and the Human Rights Act 1998. If a care order is made, the court must approve the local authority's care plan. Sometimes the threshold and disposal stages are heard separately. This can be done in order to settle disputed facts at an earlier stage (at a 'fact-finding hearing') and enable the parties to determine their positions in the light of any findings of fact made by the court.

6.5.13   A care order gives the local authority parental responsibility, sharing it with those that already have it, and enables it to implement plans for the child in accordance with its care plan. It lasts until the child is 18, unless the court brings it to an end earlier.

6.5.14   A supervision order places a duty upon the local authority to advise, assist and befriend the child. It does not give the local authority parental responsibility. It lasts for a period of one year, but can be extended upon a further application for a period up to two years.

Which court?

6.5.15 Most cases start, and will be heard, in the Family Proceedings Court. However, cases can be transferred to the county court and High Court in accordance with the Allocation and Transfer of Proceedings Order 2008, SI 2008/2836.

The conduct of care proceedings

6.5.16 The conduct of care proceedings is governed by the provisions of the Public Law Outline (see **6.5.3** and **6.5.9**).

6.5.17 A care case will usually pass through four stages:

1. *Issue and first hearing.* A local authority will commence care proceedings by completion of Form C110 and provision of key documentation:

   - Initial Social Work Statement
   - Social Work Chronology
   - Initial and Core Assessments
   - Schedule of proposed findings
   - Letter before proceedings
   - Interim care plan

   A local authority may also provide other supporting documentation (see paragraph 10 of the Public Law Outline). A children's guardian should be appointed and the child should be legally represented.

2. *Case management conference.* This is preceded by an advocates' meeting. A case management order should be prepared for the approval of the court at the case management conference.

3. *Issues resolution hearing.* This is also preceded by an advocates' meeting. A revised case management order must be prepared for the court's consideration.

4. *Final hearing.* This should resolve all outstanding issues.

Interim orders/directions hearings

6.5.18 A local authority may seek an interim care or supervision order. Such orders can be made for up to eight weeks on the first occasion and for up to four weeks on each subsequent renewal. There is no upper limit to the number of renewals that can be obtained.

6.5.19   At any stage during the proceedings, directions hearings may be held to deal with matters arising and any unexpected developments that may impact upon the case timetable. This could include changes to time estimates.

Instruction of experts

6.5.20   Any party may seek to instruct an expert in order to assist their case and/or to provide the court with material that it needs in order to come to a conclusion in the case. Parties are encouraged to use a single expert who is jointly instructed on the basis of an agreed letter of instruction.

6.5.21   Permission of the court must be sought in order to instruct an expert and the provisions of the *Practice Direction (Family Proceedings: Experts)* (2008) must be followed (see **Appendix A**).

6.5.22   Solicitors are under a duty to reveal experts' reports commissioned for the purposes of proceedings as these reports are not privileged.

Assessments

6.5.23   A parent may seek an assessment of a child under CA 1989, s.38(6). This is most commonly used where a parent is seeking a residential assessment. There is an onus on a parent to identify a suitable resource and obtain costings before making such an application. Note that since 1 October 2007 the LSC will no longer fund residential assessments, leaving the financial burden on the local authority.

6.5.24   The leading case on use of this provision is *Re G (A Minor) (Interim Care Order: Residential Assessment)* [2006] 1 AC 576.

6.6   CARE PLANS

6.6.1   When making an application for a care or supervision order, the local authority must present a care plan and before making an order, a court must approve the plan.

6.6.2   Care plans follow a format laid down in government guidance to local authorities. See Department of Health Circular, LAC 99(29) *Care Plans and Proceedings under the Children Act 1989*, at **www.dh.gov.uk**.

6.6.3   If the court does not agree with the care planning it cannot force the local authority to change their care plan, however, the court can refuse to make the order until satisfied with the care planning for the child (*Re S (Minors) (Care Order: Implementation of Care Plan); Re W (Minors) (Care Order: Adequacy of Care Plan)* [2002] 1 FLR 815.

6.7   COURT ORDERS

6.7.1   In considering the local authority's application, the court is not limited to making the order sought. It must consider the full range of orders open to it. These include all section 8 orders and special guardianship orders.

Court bundles

6.7.2   Court bundles must be produced in accordance with the *Practice Direction (Family Proceedings: Court Bundles)* [2006] 2 FLR 199.

Adoption

6.7.3   Relevant law includes:

- Adoption and Children Act (ACA) 2002, Part 1, Chapter 3
- Family Procedure (Adoption) Rules 2005, SI 2005/2795, Part 5 and Practice Directions

Placement orders

6.7.4   Where a local authority's care plan is adoption, it must apply for a placement order. Requirements are set out in ACA 2002 and the accompanying regulations.

6.7.5   A placement order is made under ACA 2002, s.21 (see Chapter 3 of ACA 2002). If made, it authorises a local authority to place a child for adoption.

6.7.6   A placement order can only be made if the child is the subject of a care order and the court is satisfied that the threshold criteria of CA 1989, s.31(2) are satisfied or the child has no parent or guardian. A court must also be satisfied that each parent or guardian has consented to the child being placed for adoption and has not withdrawn that consent, or that the parent or guardian's consent should be dispensed with.

6.7.7   An application can be made by a parent to revoke a placement order (ACA 2002, s.24), provided that the child has not been placed for adoption. A parent will need to obtain leave of the court to make such an application.

Leave will only be granted if a parent can demonstrate a change of circumstances since the placement order was made.

6.7.8 In considering whether or not to make a placement order, the welfare of the child must be the court's paramount consideration. The court must also have regard to the adoption welfare checklist contained in ACA 2002, s.1 (similar to the CA 1989 welfare checklist but with significant differences related to the issues raised by adoption), the delay principle, the 'no order' principle and the Human Rights Act 1998.

6.7.9 A placement order remains in force until it is revoked under ACA 2002, s.24, and an adoption order is made, the child marries, the child forms a civil partnership or attains the age of 18 years.

Adoption orders

6.7.10 The prospective adoptive parent(s) may apply for an adoption order. An adoption order will formally sever the relationship between the birth family and the child. Parental responsibility of the parents and any other person is extinguished and the adoptive parent(s) acquire parental responsibility for the child.

6.7.11 Where a local authority has placed a child for adoption with parental consent or under a placement order, a birth parent may apply to the court for leave to oppose the making of an adoption order. This is a two stage process. The court must be satisfied that there has been a change in circumstances since the consent was given or the placement order was made. If the court finds that there has been a change in circumstances, it must then consider, applying the welfare test, if leave should be granted.

Special guardianship orders

6.7.12 Relevant law includes:

- CA 1989 – ss.14A–14G (as inserted by ACA 2002)
- Special Guardianship Regulations 2005, SI 2005/1109
- Special Guardianship Guidance 2005 (DfES, 2005)

6.7.13 Special guardianship orders (SGOs) are made under CA 1989, ss.14A–14G (inserted by ACA 2002). The purpose of an SGO is to provide long-term security and stability for a child where other orders are not entirely suitable.

6.7.14 An SGO confers parental responsibility on the special guardian. It also allows the special guardian to exercise his or her parental responsibility to the exclusion of any other person with parental responsibility. This gives the special guardian a greater level of authority than is provided by a residence order, but does not sever family ties as with an adoption order.

6.7.15 Like a residence order, the SGO is subject to the restrictions (CA 1989, s.14C(3)) that whilst the order is in force, no person shall cause the child to be known by a new surname, or remove the child from the UK without either the written consent of every person with parental responsibility or else with the leave of the court. The special guardian can remove the child from the UK for a period of less than three months without leave or consent: this is more generous than the powers afforded under a residence order.

6.7.16 An SGO can only be varied or discharged on the application of the persons described at CA 1989, s.14D(1). The persons listed at s.14D(3) need to obtain leave of the court before they can make an application for variation or discharge. In order to obtain leave, a court must be satisfied that there has been a significant change in circumstances since the making of the SGO. Setting the hurdle for leave at this level is designed to ensure that special guardianship provides an appropriate level of permanence to the care arrangements for a child.

6.7.17 Three months' written notice must be given to the local authority by the proposed applicant of the intention to make an application to be a special guardian. Once it receives notice, the local authority must then investigate and prepare a report for the court. The report must address the suitability of the applicant to be a special guardian, other matters the local authority considers relevant and the list of matters prescribed by reg.21 of the Special Guardianship Regulations 2005 which are set out in the Schedule to the regulations.

6.7.18 CA 1989, s.14F and Part 2 of the Special Guardianship Regulations 2005 deal with special guardian support services. Section 14F places a duty on local authorities to make arrangements for the provision of services. A child who is the subject of an SGO, a special guardian, a parent or any other person who falls within a 'prescribed description' can make a request for an assessment of needs for support services and the local authority may assess. Only in the case of persons who fall within the prescribed description must the local authority carry out an assessment of that person's need for support services. The persons falling within the prescribed description comprise: a child who is looked after by the local authority or was looked after immediately prior to the making of a SGO, the special guardian or prospective special guardian of any such child, or parent of any such child.

6.7.19 If support services are to be provided, a SGO support plan should be produced. Any plan must be compiled in accordance with the Special Guardianship Regulations 2005 and Guidance.

Emergency action

6.7.20 A local authority may take emergency action through an application for an EPO (see CA 1989, s.44).

Grounds for granting an emergency protection order

6.7.21 The court must be satisfied that the test for granting an EPO is satisfied. The test is set out at s.44(1):

(a) there is reasonable cause to believe that the child is likely to suffer significant harm if –

   (i) he is not removed to accommodation provided by or on behalf of the applicant; or

   (ii) he does not remain in the place in which he is then being accommodated;

(b) in the case of an application made by a local authority –

   (i) enquiries are being made with respect to the child under section 47(1)(b); and

   (ii) those enquiries are being frustrated by access to the child being unreasonably refused to a person authorised to seek access and that the applicant has reasonable cause to believe that access to the child is required as a matter of urgency; or

(c) in the case of an application made by an authorised person –

   (i) the applicant has reasonable cause to suspect that a child is suffering, or is likely to suffer, significant harm;

   (ii) the applicant is making enquiries with respect to the child's welfare; and

   (iii) those enquiries are being frustrated by access to the child being unreasonably refused to a person authorised to seek access and the applicant has reasonable cause to believe that access to the child is required as a matter of urgency.

6.7.22 'Authorised persons' are the National Society for the Prevention of Cruelty to Children (NSPCC) and any person authorised by order of the Secretary of State to bring proceedings under CA 1989, s.31 (care proceedings).

6.7.23 On making an EPO, the court can also give directions as it considers appropriate in relation to contact between the child and any named person.

6.7.24   The court may also give directions in respect of any medical or psychiatric examination or assessment of the child and indeed it may give a direction that there is to be no examination or assessment at all or not until further order.

6.7.25   Where the court makes an EPO it may include an exclusion requirement compelling a particular person to be excluded from the home in which the child lives. The person with whom the child is to continue residing must consent to the inclusion of the exclusion requirement.

6.7.26   CA 1989, s.44B deals with the court's ability to accept undertakings from a particular person as an alternative to making an exclusion requirement. An undertaking will have the same effect as the requirement save that a power of arrest cannot be attached to it.

6.7.27   If an EPO is granted, it:

- directs any person to comply with any request to produce the child;
- allows the applicant to remove the child at any time to accommodation provided by or on behalf of the applicant and to keep the child there; and
- authorises the prevention of the child being removed from any hospital or other place of accommodation immediately before the making of the EPO.

An EPO gives the local authority parental responsibility for the child.

6.7.28   An EPO will last for up to eight days. An application for extension of the EPO can be made and if granted the extension can be made for up to a further seven days. The court must have 'reasonable cause to believe that the child concerned is likely to suffer significant harm' were it not to grant the extension.

Procedure

6.7.29   The procedure for an EPO application is as follows:

1.   Applications are made in the Family Proceedings Court.
2.   Applications are made by the local authority on Forms C1 and C11.
3.   The respondents will be the child, all persons with parental responsibility, and those persons believed to have had parental responsibility immediately prior to the making of any care order, if the child is in care.
4.   Service of application must be one day before the hearing of application.
5.   Applications can be made without notice: see the 14-point guidance

in *X Council* v. *B (Emergency Protection Order)* [2005] 1 FLR 341. This was endorsed by McFarlane J in *Re X (Emergency Protection Orders)* [2006] EWHC 510 (Fam). This guidance states that EPOs should only be made without notice if there are 'extraordinarily compelling' reasons for doing so. The guidance as a whole should be considered by the justices when deciding whether or not to grant the order.

Child assessment orders

6.7.30   See CA 1989, s.43. Child assessment orders (CAOs) were introduced as a means of ensuring that concerns about the welfare of a child could be addressed by means of a court-authorised assessment and without the need for the more drastic step of seeking an order to remove a child from his/her home. They have not been widely used but remain an option open to the local authority when it is contemplating how to safeguard the welfare of a child.

6.7.31   Section 43(1) provides:

On the application of a local authority or authorised person for an order to be made under this section with respect to a child, the court may make the order if, but only if, it is satisfied that –

(a)   the applicant has reasonable cause to suspect that the child is suffering, or is likely to suffer, significant harm;

(b)   an assessment of the state of the child's health or development, or of the way in which he has been treated, is required to enable the applicant to determine whether or not the child is suffering, or is likely to suffer, significant harm; and

(c)   it is unlikely that such an assessment will be made, or be satisfactory, in the absence of an order under this section.

6.7.32   If a CAO is made, then a person who is in a position to produce the child must do so and comply with any directions made by the court in relation to the assessment of the child.

6.7.33   A CAO shall have effect for up to seven days during which the assessment must take place. Upon an application for a CAO, a court may make an EPO instead.

Other applications

6.7.34   There are a number of other applications which may be made in public law children cases:

- to discharge a care or supervision order;

- contact – either actual contact or for permission to refuse contact;
- to place a child in secure accommodation;
- to seek a prohibited steps order, specific issue order to apply to invoke the inherent jurisdiction;
- to seek a forced marriage protection order (see the Forced Marriage (Civil Protection) Act 2007));
- for an injunction pursuant to the County Courts Act 1984, s.38 or the Protection from Harassment Act 1997.

Sources of information

6.7.35 Solicitors should be familiar with:

- *Good Practice in Child Care Cases* (2nd edn, Law Society, 2010);
- the key concepts underlying CA 1989;
- the statutory provisions as to who has parental responsibility;
- key provisions of CA 1989/ACA 2002 and regulations and guidance made thereunder;
- the Public Law Outline;
- the Public Law Outline best practice guidance;
- the range of orders open to the court which it may make on disposing of a care application;
- *Working Together to Safeguard Children* (DoE, March 2010).

6.8 TRANSPARENCY AND OPENNESS

Relevant law

6.8.1 Documents filed in care proceedings are not to be disclosed to non-parties unless one of the exemptions applies (see Family Proceedings Rules (FPR) 1991, SI 1991/1247, Part XI and Family Proceedings Courts (Children Act 1989) Rules (FPCR) 1991, SI 1991/1395, Part IIC).

6.8.2 As a result of concerns about the 'closed' nature of the family courts, regulations have been made providing for the media to have access and to report on family cases (see FPR 1991, rule 10.28 and the FPCR 1991, rule 16A). These are supported by *Practice Direction (Family Proceedings: Media Representatives: Magistrates' Courts)* [2009] 2 FLR 157 and the *Practice Direction (Family Proceedings: Media Representatives: Applications)* [2009] 2 FLR 167. Those provisions are fairly limited but will be extended under new provisions contained in the Children Schools and Families Act 2010. These provisions are yet to be brought into force.

6.8.3 Solicitors should ensure that they are aware of these provisions.

6.9 COSTS/FUNDING

6.9.1 Parents, children and persons with parental responsibility will be eligible for non-means/non-merit public funding within care proceedings.

6.9.2 Costs are rarely awarded in care cases and each party will bear their own costs. However, costs may be awarded where a party has acted unreasonably.

6.10 AFTER THE CONCLUSION OF PROCEEDINGS

6.10.1 Applications for appeals are as follows:

- Appeals from the Family Proceedings Court lie to the county court – see FPR 1991, rules 8.2A–8.2G.
- Appeals from the county court lie to the Court of Appeal – see Civil Procedure Rules 1998 (CPR), Part 52.
- Appeals from the High Court lie to the Court of Appeal – see CPR, Part 52.

6.10.2 The client should be informed of the outcome of the proceedings and the implications of any decision made by the court.

6.10.3 Clients should also be reminded of the confidential nature of proceedings and any relevant documents.

PART 7

Abduction

7.1 GENERAL

7.1.1   Solicitors must be aware of the steps that need to be taken by solicitors and their clients if a child has been abducted or is threatened with abduction.

7.1.2   Solicitors must recognise that child abduction law is a rapidly developing and highly specialist area of law and that specialist advice is absolutely essential for clients. Before agreeing to represent a client in such a case solicitors should consider whether they have the necessary knowledge and expertise and, where appropriate, the client should be referred to an alternative firm recognised for this kind of work. The Central Authority for England and Wales is a department within the Office of the Official Solicitor and Public Trustee known as The International Child Abduction and Contact Unit (ICACU). The ICACU and Reunite (see **Appendix B** for contact details) both maintain directories of solicitors who are specialists in this field. The consequences of incorrect or tardy advice can be devastating for a client, and can incur actions for negligence against the solicitors concerned.

7.2 TYPE OF OFFENCE

7.2.1   Solicitors should be aware of the difference between domestic abduction cases (i.e. within the UK) and international abduction cases, as different tests are applied by the courts.

7.2.2   Solicitors should be aware that child abduction is both a criminal and civil offence.

7.2.3   Solicitors should be aware that pursuant to the Child Abduction Act 1984, it is a criminal offence in England and Wales for any person connected with a child, to take or send the child out of the UK without the consent of any other person who has parental responsibility for the child. The exception in the Children Act (CA) 1989 is that a person with a residence order may take a child outside the jurisdiction for 28 days without the consent of all other persons with parental responsibility for the child. If a client discloses to a solicitor any threat to abduct a child, the solicitor should discuss the issue with the Law Society's Professional Ethics department (see **Appendix B** for contact details). Solicitors should consider the possibility that a criminal offence has been or will be committed and advise the client accordingly.

7.3   STATUTORY REMEDIES

7.3.1   Solicitors should be aware of the different statutory remedies, i.e. CA 1989 and the Family Law Act (FLA) 1986 for domestic cases; and the Child Abduction and Custody Act 1985, the Hague Convention on the Civil Aspects of International Child Abduction 1980 ('the Hague Convention'), the Senior Courts Act 1981 (formerly known as the Supreme Court Act 1981) and EU Council Regulation (EC) 2201/2003 ('Brussels II revised'), inter alia, for international abduction cases. Solicitors should be aware of the inter-relationship between the Hague Convention and Brussels II revised and the additional requirements in relation to abductions between all EU states (except Denmark). Solicitors should be familiar with the UK–Pakistan Judicial Protocol on Child Contact and Abduction, appended with the Guidance to Judges on the Implementation of the UK–Pakistan Judicial Protocol on Child Contact and Abduction and the guidance on Liaison between Courts in England and Wales and British Embassies and High Commissions Abroad, together with other arrangements, formal or otherwise, that the UK may have with other countries wherever possible.

7.3.2   Separate legal systems exist in Scotland and Northern Ireland and that the jurisdiction of the courts of England and Wales does not extend to these territories. Specific statutory remedies are available to deal with the cross-border movement of children.

7.3.3   Solicitors should bear in mind the court's powers pursuant to FLA 1986, namely s.33 (to order disclosure of the whereabouts of a child) and s.34 (to order the return of a child) and the inherent jurisdiction of the High Court to assist in locating and recovering an abducted child within England and Wales. Solicitors should appreciate that an order under s.33 may be directed to persons who are not a party to the proceedings (such as schools, GPs, relatives, etc) and s.34 gives a court the power to order the recovery of a child by physically taking charge of them using such force as is necessary and delivering the child to the appropriate person.

7.3.4   The police can be requested to institute a port alert for up to four weeks if there is a real and imminent risk that a child is about to be removed from

England and Wales unlawfully. No order is required. Reference should be made to *Practice Direction (Children: Removal from the Jurisdiction)* [1986] 2 FLR 89.

7.3.5   In cases of international child abduction solicitors must be able to identify when a wrongful removal or retention has occurred. Solicitors must be aware that the removal or retention has to be in breach of the left-behind parent's 'rights of custody'. The definition of that term varies from country to country.

7.3.6   When a child has been wrongfully removed to or retained in another country that is a party to the Hague Convention, the left-behind parent can make an application for the child's summary return.

7.3.7   Solicitors should be aware of the difference between an incoming child abduction case and outgoing child abduction case and be able to provide clients with appropriate advice in both situations.

7.3.8   Solicitors should also be aware of the specific rules relating to public funding in child abduction cases. In relation to an incoming case the left-behind parent is entitled to non-means, non-merits tested public funding if their case is brought to the attention of the ICACU (Community Legal Service (Financial) Regulations 2000, SI 2000/516, Part II, reg.3(1)(f)) but that a defendant's application for public funding will be subject to the usual means and merits assessment. Solicitors should also be aware that public funding may not be available in the foreign state in an outgoing case and that their client may be required to fund Hague Convention proceedings abroad.

7.3.9   All incoming cases and requests for the summary return of children presently in this jurisdiction must be issued in or immediately transferred to the High Court to be considered by a full-time High Court judge.

7.3.10   Solicitors should be aware of when it is appropriate for subject children to be interviewed by the Cafcass High Court team or separately represented.

7.3.11   In order to commence an application for a child's summary return they should immediately contact the ICACU and provide the ICACU with a completed ICACU application form. This form can be accessed from the ICACU website (**www.courtfunds.gov.uk/forms/icacu_contact.htm**). In outgoing cases the client's application will be forwarded by the ICACU to the appropriate foreign central authority with a view to Hague Convention proceedings being instituted in that country for the child(ren)'s summary return to this jurisdiction. The ICACU will then act as a point of contact with the foreign Central Authority.

7.4   MEDIATION

7.4.1   Mediation can be particularly useful and appropriate in international child abduction cases and the Hague Convention and Brussels II revised both encourage the resolution of the disputes concerning child abduction through mediation. Solicitors must be aware of the need for specialist mediators in these complex cases. Reunite runs such a scheme (see **www.reunite.org**).

PART 8

Child support

Solicitors should keep under review at all times the need to provide clients with costs information at the outset and on a regular basis. Public funding (save for legal help) is unlikely to be available.

8.1 OVERVIEW

8.1.1 Solicitors must recognise that child support law affects all family law cases where there are children, both on financial aspects and on matters of residence and contact. Variance of the child support award may undermine arrangements made in relation to the rest of the package. It may not be sufficient for the child support application to be processed by the administrative agency first, because the level of the award may be varied subsequently (in particular through a change of circumstances or variation application). It probably will not be sufficient to rely on an arrangement made at the end of the case to exclude the involvement of the agency because:

(a)   such an arrangement will probably rely on agreement of the other party which may not be forthcoming;

(b)   the arrangements may not be entirely effective even if agreed; and

(c)   practitioners must keep in mind the advantages of the administrative scheme including its lower cost and highly effective enforcement powers and services which are provided without cost.

8.1.2 Accordingly, solicitors need to be in a position to provide competent advice on:

- The jurisdiction of the administrative system.
- The definitions of 'parent with care' (PWC) and 'non-resident parent' (NRP).
- The likely amount of any calculation, bearing in mind the rules on income, pensions, the maximum calculation, further children, number of children and overnight stays.

- The availability of variations that could increase or reduce the calculation.
- The relative costs of court applications and applications to the Child Support Agency (CSA).

8.1.3 If solicitors cannot provide such competent advice, they must refer the client to a solicitor or some other agency that can do so, such that clients can make informed decisions about the options they face. Basic information sheets are available on the websites listed at **8.9.2**.

8.2 LEGISLATION

8.2.1 The Child Support Act 1991 is the main overarching Act which came into force in April 1993.

8.2.2 It has been substantially amended since, in particular by:

- Child Support Act 1995
- Social Security Act 1998
- Child Support, Pensions and Social Security Act 2000
- Child Maintenance and Other Payments Act (CMOPA) 2008

8.2.3 The last of these replaced the CSA with the Child Maintenance and Enforcement Commission (CMEC) but the CMEC operates the administrative system through its limb known as 'the Child Support Agency'. The CMEC also operates the Child Maintenance Options service which seeks to ensure that clients are aware of the option and pros and cons of a directly-managed arrangement made between paying and receiving parties.

8.3 SCHEMES

8.3.1 Solicitors need to be aware of the various formulas and when each is applicable.

1993 to March 2003

8.3.2 Applications, except in certain circumstances (see below) had to be made to the CSA. The amount was determined by a complex formula which in itself was prone to errors and there were long delays. Solicitors need not be expected to be able to work out the formula, but should be able to refer clients for appropriate advice and assistance.

Post-March 2003

8.3.3 Solicitors should be familiar with this scheme which applies to applications made on or after 3 March 2003. Only the NRP's income is taken into account, and the calculation is based on the net amount, i.e. after tax, national insurance and pension contributions are deducted, being 15% for one child, 20% for two and 25% for three or more.

8.3.4 The amount will be reduced if the NRP has one or more relevant children living with them.

Future scheme

8.3.5 Introduced by reforms under CMOPA 2008, this scheme is expected to be implemented in 2011 and will be based on the gross income of the NRP, using different percentages, namely 12%, 16% and 19%.

8.3.6 As in the previous scheme, the amount will be reduced if the NRP has one or more relevant children living with them.

The court scheme

8.3.7 This is the scheme that applies where the CSA does not have jurisdiction. The factors to be taken into account are laid down in the Matrimonial Causes Act 1973, s.25(3) and (4) and the Children Act (CA) 1989, Sched.1, para.4. However, there is judicial opinion that the determination should be influenced by the outcome that would be provided by the CSA's formula, had the CSA jurisdiction to provide a calculation (*GW* v. *RW (Financial Provision: Departure from Equality)* [2003] EWHC 611 (Fam) [74]).

8.4 JURISDICTION

8.4.1 Solicitors need to be conversant with the rules defining jurisdiction. The scheme only operates when certain conditions are met, namely:

- Parentage – a person is a parent of a child or the child is adopted.
- Age – the child must be under 16 or in full time secondary education.
- Separation – the NRP must be living in a separate household from the relevant child.
- Residence – the PWC, the NRP and the relevant child all need to be habitually resident in the UK (although there are some limited exceptions, e.g. the NRP who is abroad in the armed forces or employed by a UK-based company).

8.4.2   There are limited exceptions which may prevent the CSA becoming involved, namely:

- there was a court order in place for child maintenance which was made before 3 March 2003, in which case the court retains jurisdiction to vary the order;
- a court order has been made after 3 March 2003 and has been running for less than a year.

8.4.3   Solicitors should also be aware that under CMOPA 2008, parties are encouraged to enter into private agreements, i.e. without invoking the involvement of the CSA. However, these may not be enforceable as contracts. But note *Darke* v. *Strout* [2003] EWCA Civ 176, which confirms that there can be contractual liability on an appropriately worded agreement – even a relatively informal one – if it does not deny the intention to create legal relations.

8.4.4   Solicitors need to be aware the courts have jurisdiction in the following instances:

- if the child or parent lives abroad;
- for educational costs, e.g. school fees;
- to top up an existing maximum calculation;
- for a child over 18 still in education;
- when the parties are still in the same household;
- to make orders where the order corresponds with the terms of an agreement (and to vary such orders provided that they have not been terminated by an intervening application to the CSA).

8.4.5   In this regard solicitors also need to be aware of the court's jurisdiction under CA 1989, Sched.1.

8.5   COSTS AND LEGAL AID

8.5.1   Full public funding is not available in child support cases save for judicial reviews and hearings in the Court of Appeal on appeal from the Upper Tribunal. Solicitors can advise under the strict restrictions of Legal Help (Lower). They must make clients aware of this, but recognise that the system operates without charge both as to calculation and enforcement, a considerable saving as against court proceedings.

8.5.2   If a solicitor represents a client at a Child Support Tribunal this can only be done either as a private paying client or on a pro bono basis.

8.6 DEPARTURE AND VARIATIONS

8.6.1 Departures refer to pre-3 March 2003 cases and variations to cases from 3 March 2003 onwards.

8.6.2 These can reduce or increase the levels of payment and solicitors need to be aware of them when advising clients.

8.6.3 Factors that may reduce the level of payment are:

- significant contact costs;
- long-term illness or disability of child in NRP's household;
- NRP having ongoing liability for debts incurred for benefit of PWC or qualifying child.

8.6.4 Factors that may increase the level of payments are:

- NRP in receipt of dividends;
- NRP has assets, excluding house and business, exceeding £65,000;
- NRP has unreasonably reduced or diverted his income;
- NRP's lifestyle is inconsistent with his income.

8.7 APPEALS

8.7.1 Solicitors need to be familiar with the appeal system, particularly from an initial decision to the Child Support Appeal Tribunal (CSAT) (the First-tier tribunal).

8.7.2 Following a CSAT hearing, any party can ask for a statement of reasons: solicitors should ask for this on behalf of an unsuccessful party.

8.7.3 Permission can then be sought to appeal to the Upper Tribunal on a point of law.

8.8 COMPLAINTS

8.8.1 Solicitors must be aware of the complaints procedure. There is a strict complaints procedure, although it can be suggested to clients that they inform their MP over any dissatisfaction.

8.8.2 If a client is not satisfied with the complaints procedure, the solicitor should advise them of the procedure to involve the Independent Case Examiner, who operates an overarching Ombudsman-like function as regards the operation of the CSA.

8.9 SOURCES OF INFORMATION

8.9.1 Solicitors should be familiar with the sources of information open to them and to clients. These will include websites, books and various agencies (see **Appendices A** and **B** for details).

8.9.2 Relevant websites include:

- **www.resolution.org.uk**
- **www.cmoptions.org.uk**
- **www.csa.gov.uk**
- **www.nacsa.co.uk**

8.9.3 Among the books available are:

- *Child Support Handbook* (Child Poverty Action Group, 2010);
- *Child Support – the Legislation* (Child Poverty Action Group, 2010).

8.9.4 Relevant agencies include:

- citizens' advice bureaux;
- welfare rights organisations;
- National Association for Child Support Action.

PART 9

Schedule 1 proceedings under the Children Act 1989

Solicitors should inform their client of the likely cost of the application from the outset, and keep in mind the party's eligibility for public funding. A word of caution that any interim maintenance being made for the benefit of the child will be counted as income for the purposes of the Legal Services Commission and in the assessment of certain means tested benefits.

Practitioners should help their clients to manage these claims in a way that promotes the best interests of the children, in particular for them to maintain the strong relationships that they need with each parent. They will also need to be alert to the potential for conflict between the applicant (who may be concerned about her ability to meet her needs) and the child (who of course is the intended subject and potential beneficiary of these proceedings).

9.1 GENERAL

Scope

9.1.1 Section 15 of the Children Act (CA) 1989 states that 'Schedule 1 makes provision in relation to financial relief for children'. These proceedings are colloquially known as 'Schedule 1' proceedings and may involve:

- loans for the provision of housing costs;
- capital sums for meeting capital needs, in particular depreciating assets such as the equipping of the home, cars, computers and so on;
- provision of school fees or other educational costs and any disability costs;
- maintenance to top up maximum Child Maintenance and Enforcement Commission (CMEC) awards or general maintenance where the CMEC does not have jurisdiction;
- possibly lump sums or periodical payments for the applicant to fund the proceedings.

Who can bring proceedings?

9.1.2   A parent or guardian of a child can bring proceedings against the other parent, as can any person who has a residence order in respect of the child. Parent includes a step-parent, that is the adult who has married or been in a civil partnership with the child's natural or adoptive parent and treated the child as a child of the family – but not once the child is 18.

9.1.3   Most commonly, Schedule 1 applications are made by unmarried couples. This is because the Matrimonial Causes Act 1973 and the Civil Partnership Act 2004 are more generous than the regime under CA1989, Sched.1.

9.1.4   There is no requirement, however, that the parents should not be married or in a civil partnership. Indeed, there may well be a rise in claims by those who are married or in a civil partnership particularly given the increasing frequency and prominence of pre-nuptial and pre-registration agreements or the limitation of claims under Part III of the Matrimonial and Family Proceedings Act 1984.

9.1.5   Proceedings can only be commenced against a parent. A parent includes a party to a marriage or civil partnership and as such a claim can be initiated against a step-parent where the child is a child of the family (although not the partner or former partner of a cohabitant).

9.1.6   The manner in which the child is conceived is irrelevant. No regard is taken of whether or not the child was planned, or was born as a result of a casual encounter or the product of a stable long term relationship.

9.1.7   Financial provision is for a child. A child is defined as a person under the age of 18, though the provision can be extended beyond the child reaching 18, and into tertiary education, potentially including a short period thereafter.

9.1.8   A child over 16 can make an application in their own right but only for the variation or revival of a previous periodical payments order. A child over 18 can also make an application but only if they are in education and their parents are separated. Public funding should always be considered, as children, even adult children in education, are less likely to have sufficient resources to meet the legal fees.

9.1.9   A Schedule 1 claim may be bought in circumstances where the parents are still living together (and hence there is no non-resident parent to enable an application to the CMEC). This may provide a useful mechanism to secure financial support in claims of modest value and whereby it is not immediately possible to afford two separate households.

9.1.10   Practitioners should be aware that the court, when making, varying or discharging a residence order, can make orders under Schedule 1 of its own motion even if no application under this Schedule has been made to the court. This power seems to be applied infrequently, if at all.

Parental responsibility

9.1.11   Practitioners should check whether their client has parental responsibility. If the parents were unmarried when the child was born, then the father may not have parental responsibility, unless they have already entered into a parental responsibility agreement, or the child was registered or re-registered after 30 November 2003 and the father was named on the birth certificate, or there is a shared residence order in place.

9.1.12   If the father does not have parental responsibility, the practitioner should advise him to enter into a parental responsibility agreement or where the mother does not agree whether he should apply for an order under CA 1989, s.4.

9.1.13   In any event, a Schedule 1 claim can be made against a father regardless of whether or not the father has parental responsibility. A claim can also be made against any parent regardless of the level, or quality, of the relationship that they have with the child.

Paternity

9.1.14   Practitioners should remember that in any case where parentage is an issue the court can direct the taking of samples from a child for the purpose of DNA testing.

9.1.15   Best practice is to endeavour to obtain consent to the DNA test in order to reduce costs. If an agreement can not be reached then an application for a declaration of parentage under the Family Law Act 1986, s.55A should be made.

9.1.16   A word of caution that declaration of parentage applications are heard in open court, and therefore will be in the public domain, unlike Children Act applications, which the public are unable to attend.

Jurisdiction of the Child Maintenance Enforcement Commission

9.1.17   The Child Support Act 1991, s.8(3) restricts the court from making a periodical payment order to a narrow band of cases. Therefore if your client qualifies to apply to the CMEC and an agreement has not been reached between the parties that the court should deal with child maintenance instead, then the court can only make a periodical payment order in the following circumstances:

- for educational costs;
- for disability costs;
- for top-up maintenance to the CMEC maintenance calculation where the respondent's net income is over (currently) £104,000 per annum.

9.1.18   Clients should be advised immediately to apply to the CMEC for child support if the non-resident parent (NRP) is not earning over £104,000 per annum and where both parents and the child are resident in the UK.

9.1.19   Further, even where the NRP is earning over £104,000 per annum it is advisable to commence an application to the CMEC at the outset so as to enable a maximum assessment to be secured and thereafter enable the court to exercise its 'top-up' jurisdiction. An applicant's claims under Schedule 1 will be restricted at a final hearing in the event that a maximum assessment has not been obtained.

9.1.20   Practitioners should note that the CMEC does not have jurisdiction if the NRP is not living in England and Wales. However, there are exceptions where the NRP is a member of the armed forces, is employed by the civil service or works for a UK-based company, whose employees work outside the UK, but whose payment arrangements are in the UK.

9.1.21   The CMEC also does not have jurisdiction to make any provision for the NRP. The NRP (or a parent with shared care, but considered by the CMEC to be non-resident) can however have recourse to Schedule 1.

9.1.22   A claim for a lump sum can still be applied for under CA 1989, Sched.1 even if the CMEC has jurisdiction. The CMEC ceases to have jurisdiction when a child attains 16 or, if later, ends secondary education (with a cut-off at the age of 19).

9.2   PROCEEDINGS

Alternative dispute resolution

9.2.1   Consideration should always be given as a matter of good general practice to alternatives to litigation (see **Part 2**). The importance of this consideration is often heightened in Schedule 1 proceedings given the potential costs of litigation, particularly so when considering that the applicant's claim is not for capital outright but for the provision of income needs and for a home during the child's minority. Even in a case whereby the applicant secures a legal fees order, and save in the cases where there is considerable and notable wealth, the available capital for provision for a home is inevitably reduced through the costs of litigation.

Where are proceedings issued?

9.2.2 Proceedings under Schedule 1 can be issued in any county court, or at the High Court. The magistrates' court has limited jurisdiction to order lump sums of up to £1,000 and cannot deal with other matters such as secured periodical payments, settlements or transfers of property.

9.2.3 Any case which also involves potential property proceedings (see **9.4.6– 9.4.15**), should be issued in a court that has jurisdiction under both Schedule 1 and the Trusts of Land and Appointment of Trustees Act 1996 given that the proceedings are likely to be conjoined.

9.2.4 In any case involving an international element, consideration should be given to whether or not a claim can be made in an alternative jurisdiction and if so whether or not it is advantageous for your client to do so. This is most commonly considered in the context of securing a more favourable jurisdiction for the applicant. A respondent may wish to commence proceedings against themselves in an overseas jurisdiction or in England and Wales (depending on which is the less generous jurisdiction).

9.2.5 International jurisdiction matters should be considered at the outset, as a matter of priority and clearly before issuing any proceedings. This note of caution extends to issuing any proceedings of any kind whatsoever (including those relating to the welfare or upbringing of a child) given the possibility that such proceedings (even if not directly akin to Schedule 1) may be considered related or ancillary such as to either prevent a later Schedule 1 application or cause a conflict of competing jurisdictions to arise.

9.2.6 For a fuller analysis of the jurisdiction issues in relation to Schedule 1 claims, reference should be made to *Claims under Schedule 1 to the Children Act 1989* (Resolution, 2009) (notably chapter 8). Particular attention should also be given to the risks of losing the chance of a constructive settlement through pre-emptive issue of opportunistic proceedings in a different jurisdiction.

Application procedure

9.2.7 The following procedure applies:

1.   Applications should be made to the court on Form C1, along with the supplementary Form C10 in which the applicant sets out information in support of their financial application, and a Form C1A, which sets out the applicant's financial circumstances and a schedule of their living expenses.

2.   The initial application forms provide summary information only and it is likely that it will be necessary for further information to be supplied, particularly financial information (see disclosure at **9.2.15–9.2.19**). That said, care must be taken when completing these forms particularly given that this may be the only information on which the case is assessed (at least initially) and furthermore to ensure that such disclosure is consistent with any future more detailed disclosure. This applies as much to the applicant who, as well as providing a summary of their financial position, must give an indication of their needs.

3.   If there have already been proceedings concerning the child in question, it may be advisable to issue on Form C2 so that the Schedule 1 proceedings are dealt with by the same judge as the previous proceedings if at all possible.

4.   The relevant fee must be enclosed with the forms. Practitioners should be aware that a fee exemption may be relevant if your client has a limited income.

5.   The forms can be found at **www.hmcourts-service.gov.uk**

9.2.8   Once the case is issued:

1.   The court will provide the issued copies to the applicant in order that they can serve on the respondent the sealed copies of the above, along with notice to the parties of the hearing date on Form C6 and an acknowledgement of service on Form C7. A blank Form C10A should also be provided for the respondent to complete.

2.   Once the applicant has served the documents, they should file confirmation of service on Form C9. The respondent must acknowledge the documents within 14 days of receipt.

Court hearings

9.2.9   The normal process will be a first directions appointment (FDA), followed, if agreed, by a hearing held as if it were a financial dispute resolution (FDR) appointment, followed by a final hearing. However, practitioners may find that matters are insufficiently clear by the time of the FDA for meaningful directions to be given which may necessitate a further visit to court, for example:

•   FDA, e.g. when directions for exchange of Forms E may well be given;

- 'first appointment' style hearing when orders for disclosure on those documents may be ordered;
- FDR-style hearing;
- final hearing.

9.2.10   Practitioners should aim to have discussions at an early stage to agree what disclosure should be given and to timetable the case so as to minimise the number of attendances at court where possible.

9.2.11   Should the matter be compromised the proceedings will need to be dealt with. The application can be withdrawn with leave of the court, but, more likely, a consent order will need to be submitted and approved. For the reasons set out below, it may also be desirable for an agreement reached without proceedings being issued to be embodied in a consent order.

9.2.12   There is no defined procedure for the lodging of a consent order under Schedule 1. The court will inevitably require details of the parties' means when considering proposed terms of compromise. If proceedings have already been issued then the court file may already have the requisite claim forms, including the financial claim forms (and potentially a Form E). Even in these circumstances the court may be aided by the provision of a summary of the financial and factual information. This could be provided on either application Forms C10 and C10A, or on a Form M1 (statement of information in ancillary relief proceedings) particularly where the ancillary relief procedure has been adopted or in a summary format (potentially accompanied by an schedule of assets/income).

9.2.13   If proceedings have not been initiated, then it is likely that a Form C1 or C2 will need to be issued, at the least so as to secure a case number. It may be feasible, depending upon the cooperation of the court in question, to in part forgo the procedural requirements set out above, and lodge the proposed terms together with a financial summary for consideration. This would potentially require an application to the court, either by way of a written application or a short hearing.

9.2.14   It may be particularly important to take this step when acting for a respondent where provision of housing is in issue. An applicant is prohibited from repeat applications for housing but if there has been no court order to confirm the housing provision then there is no prohibition on the applicant seeking a second arrangement.

Disclosure

9.2.15 CA 1989 is primarily concerned with welfare decisions. It has not been designed for financial disputes and therefore practitioners may want to adopt the ancillary relief procedure in conducting their case. If so, this can either be established by agreement at the outset, or alternatively the FDA may be used by the court to lay down directions for disclosure and future case management.

9.2.16 At the issue of proceedings the applicant will have already provided a Form C10A. However, this form is limited in its use as the disclosure provided is brief. Often the respondent will not have provided a statement of means prior to the first hearing and that may mean that little progress will be made and a further directions appointment probably needed, increasing the time and costs expended on the application for both parties.

9.2.17 The Court of Appeal in *Morgan* v. *Hill* [2006] EWCA Civ 1602 said that the courts are content to adopt disclosure by way of Form E in Schedule 1 cases. Further, where agreement can be reached it may be useful to adopt, by consent, the full ancillary relief type timetable listing the first appointment sufficiently far in advance to potentially enable it to be used as an FDR-style hearing (or at least a date in the future to allow the disclosure process to be concluded so far as is possible) and potentially providing for questionnaires, replies, etc. For such a procedure to be adopted, the court may require that an application is issued and thereafter a consent order agreed and lodged. This case management may be secured by either submitting a paper application by consent or by a short hearing before the court seeking approval of the proposed directions.

9.2.18 Even in the event that the ancillary relief procedure is adopted, disclosure may not be the same as in ancillary relief proceedings. Precise knowledge of the respondent's means, in particular, is not needed by the court which is generally more concerned with understanding the lifestyle of the respondent. A broad understanding of wealth and lifestyle only will be required by the court in high-worth cases, albeit that in 'needs-based' cases greater detail may ordinarily be required to enable the court to assess just what can be done so as to balance up the financial hardship of separation. The 'millionaires' defence may still be employed where relevant in Schedule 1 proceedings.

9.2.19 Practitioners should note that there is no equivalent in Schedule 1 to s.37 of the Matrimonial Causes Act 1973 dealing with avoidance of transactions and freezing injunctions and hence that such an application in Schedule 1 proceedings should be made under the Civil Procedure Rules 1998.

Media

9.2.20   Practitioners should be aware that since 27 April 2009 the media can now attend all family court hearings, except where those hearings are for conciliation/negotiation. Accordingly, it is important to ensure the client is aware of this. Equally, it is important, if the ancillary relief procedure is adopted, that consideration is given to excluding the media at any FDR-style hearing.

9.2.21   Only accredited press members can attend and members of the public are still excluded from the hearings.

9.2.22   However, even though the press can attend there is still a prohibition on publishing to the public at large, or any section of the public, material intended to or likely to identify a child as being involved in proceedings, or the address or school of any such child. This prohibition is limited to the duration of the proceedings but the court should consider whether the protection should continue thereafter.

9.2.23   There are certain circumstances where the court can be asked not to allow the press to be at the hearing, or part of the hearing.

9.3   COSTS

9.3.1   Practitioners should be mindful that the 'no order as to costs' principle implemented by the Family Proceedings (Amendment) Rules 2006, SI 2006/352 does not apply in Schedule 1 cases.

9.3.2   Practitioners can apply during the proceedings for provision for legal costs either as interim periodical payments or as an interim lump sum. However, this area is in its infancy and specialist advice is likely to be required.

9.4   COURT POWERS

Children Act 1989, Schedule 1, para.4(1) and (2)

9.4.1   In deciding whether to exercise its powers under CA 1989, Sched.1, para.4(1) or (2), the court must have regard to all the circumstances of the case including (para.4(1)):

    (a)   the income, earning capacity, property and other financial resources which each person ... has or is likely to have in the foreseeable future;

    (b)   the financial needs, obligation and responsibilities which each person ... has or is likely to have in the foreseeable future;

(c)   the financial needs of the child
(d)   the income, earning capacity (if any), property and other financial resources of the child;
(e)   any physical or mental disability of the child
(f)   the manner in which the child was being, or was expected to be, educated or trained.

9.4.2   Where the court has freedom to decide (because the CMEC does not have jurisdiction or because a maximum assessment is in place), a carer's allowance can be included when assessing any periodical payments award. The problem that the court is faced with is that there is a perceived conflict between identifying an award for the child and awarding the mother. The court has suggested that in relevant cases this perceived conflict could perhaps be addressed by securing separate representation for the child.

9.4.3   An issue that a practitioner should discuss with any applicant is that the applicant cannot put aside as savings any money provided by the respondent. The approach has built up that the applicant can save any of their own income (once any child-care costs have been discharged) but the applicant should be advised that any savings or income that they have accrued during their child's minority may be counted against them in any variation application.

9.4.4   There is however no statutory provision that the applicant must apply their own resources to meet accommodation or income needs either on an originating application or on subsequent variation. Each case is fact specific.

9.4.5   For a fuller analysis of these factors, reference should be made to *Claims under Schedule 1 to the Children Act 1989* (Resolution, 2009) (notably chapters 4 and 5).

Provision for housing, including settlement of property and the transfer of property

9.4.6   Schedule 1 proceedings are not the appropriate forum to resolve issues relating to financial interests in, or claims to, real property. If the applicant asserts a beneficial interest in a property then such claim should be pursued under the Trust of Land and Appointment of Trustees Act 1996. The court in Schedule 1 proceedings is not permitted to award the applicant a beneficial interest in a property, or even declare whether or not such interest is held or shared between the applicant and the respondent.

9.4.7   In the event that there are property issues to be resolved, then both claims should be issued and heard in tandem. This may influence where the property claim is issued so as to ensure that the court also has jurisdiction under Schedule 1. The court has stated that the Schedule 1 proceedings should have lead status given the potential for a more generous award (albeit a discretionary rather than declaratory award, at least in the interim). That said, it remains the case that it will be essential to secure the declaratory order in addition to the discretionary award such that any order can properly record how the beneficial interest is shared (if at all), and hence what part of the property is provided on trust such that it must revert to the respondent and what part is the applicant's outright and hence can be retained.

9.4.8   Housing is generally provided for by a settlement or transfer of property order, but can include a transfer of a tenancy. Schedule 1 has limited jurisdiction provisions, but the court to date has interpreted para.14 as a prohibition on a settlement or transfer of property order where the child resides abroad.

9.4.9   The respondent is entitled to the property on reversion, normally when the child reaches the age of 18 or completes full-time education or ceases to be dependent (the precise arrangements are agreed or determined on a case-by-case basis). Provision of housing has, however, included housing during tertiary education and has occasionally extended beyond such for a relatively short and defined period of time.

9.4.10   The court has suggested that as the respondent is entitled to the reversion, s/he should have some veto as to unsuitable investments. The matter of whether or not a future alternative or replacement property should also be considered, including who should bear the costs of sale, purchase and move. Consideration should be given to whether or not it is appropriate to include provisions to take effect should the applicant cohabit or (re)marry. Equally, on termination of any trust arrangement, consideration should be given as to whether or not it is appropriate to grant the applicant an option to purchase and if so on what basis (e.g. a staged buy-out option is yet a further alternative).

9.4.11   There have been many methods adopted by the courts to specify how a property could be held, for example, trustees appointed by the applicant and the respondent, the applicant holding the house in their sole name, with a charge that the proceeds of sale are to go to the respondent. There have been also situations where the respondent can own the property outright and grant a license or lease to the applicant giving them a right to occupy the property during the child's minority. The tax consequences of the arrangement are likely to be an influencing, if not a dominant, factor (see **9.4.14**).

9.4.12   Only one property order may be made. Consideration should therefore be given as to when the application should be made if the circumstances are such that the respondent's means are likely to increase substantially, and it is foreseeable that a more appropriate property award may be made at a later date. Property provision in the interim could be made by consent and on the understanding that such provision did not constitute the final satisfaction of the property claim (and hence was not recorded in an order) or alternatively potentially by the payment of rent/mortgage payments through a periodical payments order. The respondent may however be reluctant to enter into such an arrangement and ensure any settlement or transfer of property is embodied in a court order as a settlement or transfer of property order such that it is not open to the applicant to revisit the property claims on a subsequent application.

9.4.13   In addition to the property itself, consideration should be given to the costs of acquisition, including stamp duty and other immediate costs. This can be dealt with by way of a lump sum order (which may also provide for further costs associated with acquiring, renovating and outfitting a new home): see **9.4.16–9.4.18**. In addition, if the applicant is to make a financial contribution to the purchase (either initially on purchase or subsequently – such as by improving the property or contributing to any mortgage payments) then it should be established from the outset as to whether or not such contributions are intended to lead to the applicant acquiring a beneficial interest in the property and, if so, on what basis. A failure to regulate this (even if only to confirm that no beneficial interest will be acquired) may lead to disputed trust of land proceedings upon the property no longer being required for the child (or potentially even at an earlier stage).

9.4.14   The practitioner should bear in mind that how the property is held may have vastly differing tax implications when the property is sold. Tax advice should therefore be obtained before drawing up any proposed terms of compromise, drafting any consent order or prior to any contested hearing and ideally obtained early in the process so that each side agrees the basis upon which the discussions are advancing.

9.4.15   As can be seen it is not only the quantum of the property fund that is important. The minutia of the arrangements should also be considered at an early stage, and certainly when nearing agreement or adjudication, it is useful to start exchanging draft documents such that the above issues are not overlooked.

Lump sum order

9.4.16   Lump sum orders make provision for specific items of expenditure. Commonly, these are employed to provide money to the applicant for the cost of furnishing or renovating a property, including white goods, or for the cost of a family car. There is, however, no statutory restriction on the purposes for which a lump sum may be sought, and indeed a lump sum may be sought for expenditure which has already been incurred. However, the courts have rejected claims where the spending relates to revenue expenditure and the CMEC would have had jurisdiction.

9.4.17   Unlike property-related orders, there can be repeat lump sum claims/ orders. Further the court can order a series of lump sums, or a lump sum payable by instalments, in which case the number of instalments, amount and the date can be subject to a subsequent variation application. A lump sum should not be used, however, to make further property provision where there has already been a settlement or transfer of property order.

9.4.18   A lump sum (given that it is designed to meet specific expenditure) does not revert back to the respondent and hence is a once-and-for-all payment. This applies irrespective of whether the item acquired continues to have financial value upon the end point of the arragement. Accordingly, consideration should be given to the time frame for any lump sum such that, so far as is possible, the applicant is not provided with an asset which they are able to retain irrespective of the fact that the child is no longer being provided for. An example of this would be the provision for renewal of a car, which should be timed such that a new car is not provided shortly before the child's dependency comes to an end.

Periodical payments/secured periodical payments

9.4.19   These are a claim for ongoing maintenance for the benefit of the child, and can include an element attributable to a 'carer's allowance' (that is costs that do not relate so much to the outlay directly on the child but which are incurred by the carer of the child in meeting his/her day-to-day expenses). An award may incidentally benefit siblings who are not the subject children of a claim. Where, however, there are multiple children and two or more fathers then consideration should be given to whether multiple claims should be issued and such claims conjoined. A specific approach has been laid down by the courts to manage this situation.

9.4.20   According to CA 1989, Sched.1, para.3(1), the claim for periodical payments in the first instance should not extend beyond the child's 17th birthday unless the court thinks it right but in any event it shall not extend beyond the child's 18th birthday. This provision does not apply, however, (para.2(2)) if the child is or will be receiving further education or special circumstances apply. Orders are therefore on occasion made to extend into tertiary education and for a very short period of adjustment thereafter.

9.4.21 Remember that if the CMEC has jurisdiction then this prevents a claim under CA 1989, Sched.1 for periodical payments unless the circumstances that were mentioned before apply (that is – broadly – that the order is for educational or disability costs or is to top up a maximum assessment or, finally, that the order is in line with an agreement reached between the parties).

9.4.22 It should also be noted that in circumstances where the CMEC has jurisdiction but the parties agree that the court can proceed to make an award, either party can apply to the CMEC for an assessment after the expiry of 12 months from the date of the order (or – arguably if later – the variation order). Accordingly, there will always remain an element of risk of an enforced CMEC future variation/assessment in circumstances where an award is agreed or determined which differs from the likely CMEC assessment.

9.4.23 Where the court retains jurisdiction to award periodical payments it is likely to be assisted by provision of an estimate of child support maintenance that would be assessed by CMEC (particularly where the annual net income is less that £104,000 per annum). The court is, however, not obliged to follow such an assessment when making its award. A child support maintenance assessment calculator is located on the CSA website below and as such an estimate assessment can be easily produced. That said, it is important to provide evidence of not only the results of the estimated assessment but also the criteria applied in obtaining such results such that the other party and the court are aware of the basis on which the assessment is predicated (the net income applied, the element, if any, of shared care deductions, and whether the potential for any variation application has been factored in, etc.). Currently, the website produces only the answers and hence the 'input' information should be printed and collated as the calculation is progressed.

9.4.24 The court may consider backdating the periodical payments award. It can only do so to the date of the application, save where there is a CMEC assessment, in which case the court may backdate to the later of six months before the application, or the date on which the current assessment took effect.

9.4.25 For the reasons set out above, the CMEC assessment secured before a 'top-up' application must be a maximum assessment, and hence if it appears that this is not the case, then clarification should be obtained as to why this is so. It may initially appear that the assessment is not a maximum assessment but this may simply be due to a reduction in the assessment arising from an element of shared care. Such deductions do not prevent an application under Schedule 1. Clarification should be sought from the CMEC where such circumstances arise therefore as the best evidence is likely to be from the letter confirming the calculations. Take care that such a calculation will not be overtaken by a last minute re-calculation following a change of circumstances, as if at the time of the hearing there is no maximum assessment, the court cannot make a periodical payments order without agreement. It may be that an order by consent should be made early in the proceedings which can then be varied.

9.4.26 Provision for costs of education (most commonly school fees) can be awarded irrespective of whether the income of the paying party falls below the CMEC threshold of £104,000 net per annum.

9.4.27 As well as considering the applicant's and respondent's income position, advice should be given on the availability of welfare benefits, including, but not limited to, tax credits. This is particularly relevant where the family structure has changed such that previously unavailable benefits may now be obtainable or a revised benefit assessment conducted.

9.4.28 It is worth investigating life insurance to be taken out by the respondent in case of premature death, to cover the periodical payments from the date of death until the end of dependence.

9.4.29 An order for periodical payments terminates if the parties reconcile and live together for more than six months (CA 1989, Sched.1, para.3(3)).

Interim orders/variation

9.4.30 The court has the power to make interim maintenance orders, and it appears increasingly accepted that these can contain an element for legal fees for the applicant. Lump sum orders may also be obtained on an interim basis.

9.4.31 Orders for periodical payments can be varied or discharged. Orders for the settlement or transfer of property can be made once only. Contrast this to orders for lump sums which are not limited such that there may be more than one lump sum, lump sums payable by instalments or more than one application for a lump sum(s).

9.5 ON CONCLUSION OF THE CASE

9.5.1 Practitioners should remind their clients that the Court of Appeal in *Re P (Child: Financial Provision)* [2003] 2 FLR 865 stated that any money received by way of maintenance for the child must be used by the end of each year and not used for savings.

9.6 SOURCES OF INFORMATION

The following websites and publications provide further guidance (see also **Appendices A** and **B**):

- **www.hmcourts-service.gov.uk/HMCSCourtFinder/ FormFinder.do**
- **www.csa.gov.uk**
- **www.childmaintenance.org**
- *Claims under Schedule 1 to the Children Act 1989* (Resolution, 2009).

PART 10

Proceedings for dissolution, divorce, judicial separation or nullity

10.1 GENERAL

Scope

10.1.1 This section covers all applications for divorce, judicial separation or nullity, unless otherwise specified, and dissolution of civil partnerships.

In all matters

10.1.2 Solicitors should always bear in mind the following:

1. Family issues often go to the heart of people's religious, cultural or personal beliefs.

2. The impact of, for example, the contents of a divorce petition or correspondence upon other issues such as children and financial applications.

3. The cultural and/or religious implications of divorce should be considered, for example, the question of obtaining a 'get' (a divorce under Jewish religious law) or a 'talaq' (a divorce under Islamic religious law). To some clients of particular faiths, obtaining a divorce according to their religion may be as important as, or more important than, a civil divorce. Certain faiths have stringent rules, set a timetable for the civil divorce or only allow a husband to apply. Solicitors must consider these issues when they are given instructions and take such steps as they reasonably can in the civil divorce to help clients to obtain a religious divorce. In this context solicitors must be aware of the effect of the Divorce (Religious Marriages) Act 2002. Solicitors should also refer to **www.gettingyourget.co.uk** which offers guidance.

4. A forced marriage (that is, a marriage to which the consent of each party is not freely given, but is obtained by duress) may raise issues

beyond those normally found in dissolution. Solicitors should be aware of the problem, and if necessary refer to experts in the field or seek assistance from agencies with experience of dealing with victims of this form of abuse. If a solicitor is approached in connection with an individual who has been removed from England and Wales, they should contact the Forced Marriage Unit, a joint initiative by the Home Office and Foreign and Commonwealth Office at **fmu@fco.gov.uk** (see **Appendix B**).

5.   Issues that arose during the marriage, which are irrelevant to the evidence of irretrievable breakdown of the marriage but which may impact on children or ancillary relief issues, such as allegations of unreasonable behaviour, should be dealt with in separate correspondence.

Judicial separation or nullity

10.1.3   Although applications for judicial separation or nullity are rare, there will be circumstances in which it will be impossible to obtain a divorce or where it is appropriate to obtain a decree of nullity or judicial separation. These may, in particular, be appropriate where clients have strong religious and/or cultural reasons for not wishing to divorce or in cases when a divorce decree would cause a loss of pension rights, or where parties have not been married for 12 months.

10.1.4   Where an application for judicial separation is appropriate, solicitors should discuss with clients the possible extra expense of obtaining a divorce after a decree of judicial separation. The ramifications of obtaining a judicial separation also need to be discussed, most particularly the ramifications in relation to pension benefits and the death of one of the parties to the marriage after judicial separation. Solicitors should also explain that the respondent in a suit for judicial separation could issue an application for divorce in any event, provided the parties have been married for 12 months.

10.1.5   In cases where there is a choice of divorce or nullity solicitors should discuss with clients the additional expense of obtaining a decree of nullity, rather than one of divorce, due to the need for a court hearing.

Civil partnerships

10.1.6   Same sex couples who have registered their partnership can apply to dissolve their partnership. Such partnerships can only be dissolved on the ground of irretrievable breakdown. The process for dissolution of civil partnership is the same as for divorce. The only exception is adultery which is a specific term relating to heterosexual sex and therefore cannot be used. In such circumstances unreasonable behaviour may be used.

10.2 BEFORE ISSUING PROCEEDINGS

10.2.1 Before the start of proceedings the petitioner's solicitors should do the following:

- Note that there is an absolute bar upon presenting a divorce petition within one year of the date of the marriage.
- In appropriate circumstances, consider which country or countries are the appropriate jurisdictions to issue proceedings for dissolution, and if appropriate (see in particular EU Council Regulation (EC) 2201/2003), which is the most advantageous. In deciding the appropriate jurisdiction, solicitors should consider all factors including the remedies available and the nature and location of assets.
- Notify the respondent's solicitors (or respondent where unrepresented) of the intention to commence proceedings at least seven days in advance, unless there are good reasons for not doing so (see **1.11.1**);
- Provide the respondent's solicitors (or respondent where unrepresented) with the fact or facts on which the petition is to be based and the particulars, with a view to coming to an agreement.
- Obtain the marriage certificate and check that the marriage of the parties is recognised in this country.
- Advise clients to confirm that a decree granted here will be recognised in the country in which they will live, so far as is practicable.

10.2.2 Solicitors should ensure that a list of approved translators is kept in the office so that a speedy and accurate translation of a marriage certificate can be obtained if necessary.

10.3 THE PETITION

10.3.1 In drafting the petition the following guidelines should be followed:

1. Where the divorce proceedings are issued on the basis of adultery:

   (a) petitioners should be advised not to name co-respondents as there is no need to do so in law (unless a petitioner wishes to claim costs against the co-respondent);

   (b) respondents should be advised that if they do not want to defend the proceedings an admission of adultery on the acknowledgement of service is likely to be sufficient evidence. There should be no need for separate confession statements.

2. Where the divorce proceedings are issued on the basis of unreasonable behaviour, petitioners should be encouraged only to include brief particulars sufficient to satisfy the court and not to include any reference to children.

3. In all cases solicitors should ensure that all parties, particularly those that are not represented, understand that the reason for the breakdown of the marriage has no bearing on either the financial outcome or the arrangements for the children.

4. In all cases costs should not be sought lightly or routinely. Solicitors should consider carefully with clients the possible aggravating effect of claiming costs from respondents and such claims should only be made when it is considered appropriate.

5. It might be considered appropriate to make a claim for costs in the petition, for example:

> The Petitioner will not seek the costs of the petition against the Respondent unless the Respondent fails to file an Acknowledgement of Service within seven days confirming he/she does not intend to defend the proceedings or otherwise fails to cooperate in the efficient progress of the divorce.

5. In all cases solicitors should explain what an application for financial relief is and why it is necessary to include it in the petition.

10.3.2 Solicitors advising a petitioner should check that the petition is completed accurately by checking the information contained in the marriage certificate. Common errors include the names of the parties or the place of marriage not being shown exactly as they appear in the marriage certificate.

10.3.3 Where a petitioner is being advised under Legal Help and Help at Court, care needs to be taken on obtaining up-to-date and original evidence of all income received if applying to be exempt from all court fees. Failure to do so may cause delay.

10.4   THE STATEMENT OF ARRANGEMENTS FOR CHILDREN

10.4.1 The 'statement of arrangements' form is an important document and must be completed carefully. The court cannot fulfil its statutory obligations unless this form is completed fully.

10.4.2 Before filing the statement of arrangements for children:

- A copy should normally be sent to the respondent's solicitors (or respondent where unrepresented) for approval and a reasonable time should be allowed for reply.
- The other party's signature should be obtained where possible.

- Only information necessary to state the arrangements being made for the children should be included.
- Solicitors should discuss with clients the arrangements being proposed for the children to ensure that the interests of the children are not overlooked. Clients should be encouraged to discuss and agree arrangements for parenting with their spouses where appropriate and when it is safe to do so.
- If at the time the petition is issued a parenting plan has been agreed by both parties, it should be attached to the statement of arrangements for children.

10.5   SERVICE

10.5.1   The respondent is usually served by post by the court office. The respondent may be served personally but not personally by the petitioner and not on a Sunday without the permission of the court. The petitioner cannot proceed until service is proved.

10.5.2   The respondent is served with the petition, a court form entitled 'Notice of Proceedings and Acknowledgement of Service' and a copy of any statement of arrangements. Any co-respondent is served with the petition and the 'Notice of Proceedings and Acknowledgement of Service'.

10.5.3   If service is either very difficult or even impossible the petitioner can apply for one of the following orders:

- an order for substituted service;
- an order dispensing with service;
- an order deeming service if there is evidence that the respondent has received the papers.

Specific rules apply to service on minors and on patients.

10.5.4   Service out of the jurisdiction is potentially complex and errors may have serious consequences including losing jurisdiction to another country.

10.6   ACTING FOR THE RESPONDENT

10.6.1   If solicitors are acting for a respondent who has received a divorce petition where there is a claim for costs, it is quite appropriate to write to the petitioner's solicitors to ask whether they are prepared not to pursue the claim for costs, or alternatively, to specify a limited figure for costs that can be agreed if the divorce proceeds undefended. Where the petitioner is receiving advice under Legal Help and Help at Court it may be possible to agree not to pursue the claim for costs unless the contractual or statutory charge applies. However, if such a letter is to be written it is important to consider whether the petitioner or their solicitor might use the letter in evidence in an affidavit for deemed service. Care should be taken in subsequent correspondence. Marking the letter 'without prejudice' may not be sufficient to prevent this as it can still be used. The fact that a petition has been received does not attract privilege.

10.6.2 If the respondent to a petition based on unreasonable behaviour disagrees with the allegations made, it is appropriate to write on the acknowledge-ment of service that the allegations are not admitted. However, if it is indicated that the allegations are denied, a court might take that as an indication of a defence and not allow the matter to proceed under the special procedure.

10.6.3 The filing of answers and cross-petitions should be discouraged unless there are good reasons for doing so. Solicitors acting for respondents who are unhappy with the allegations made can record their client's concerns in correspondence so that the petitioner is aware of them. Where clients wish to defend allegations made in divorce petitions because they may be relevant on determination of ancillary relief or on children issues, the parties should be encouraged to enter into agreements whereby respond-ents do not accept the particulars but will not defend the main suit, and whereby petitioners will agree that respondents are free to raise their concerns afresh in the ancillary relief or children proceedings. This agree-ment should be made within correspondence.

10.6.4 Respondents to petitions must be discouraged from filing another petition in the same or another court unless for very good reason, for example substantial delay in proceeding with the originating petition.

10.6.5 Solicitors should be aware that in divorce cases where immigration compli-cations also arise, cross-petitions by clients who have suffered abuse or violence may be necessary so that they have an opportunity to give their explanation of why their marriage failed. Solicitors should consider cross-petitions in such cases because a client's immigration application to stay in the country may be prejudiced by allegations made against him or her by the applicant in the divorce petition. In such cases a referral to a specialist in immigration law might be appropriate.

10.7 APPLICATION FOR DECREE NISI

10.7.1 If the decree nisi is undefended the petitioner files an affidavit of evidence on a standard Form M7 together with the form requesting special procedure directions. The District Judge will consider whether the petitioner has approved the contents of the petition, any claim for costs and, where there are children, whether the court should exercise its powers. If all is well notification of the date for pronouncement will be sent to all parties. If not satisfied the judge may:

- give the petitioner the opportunity of filing further evidence;
- direct that costs may be dealt with upon receiving an application; or
- give directions as regards children.

Neither party is required to attend when the decree nisi is pronounced.

10.8   DEFENDED HEARINGS

10.8.1   Notice of the desired place of trial, number and place of residence of witnesses is served on the other party by the party applying. Notice can be given by either the petitioner or respondent. The recipient of the notice responds within eight days with the desired place of trial and number and residence of witnesses. Directions for trial are filed and the District Judge will give directions for trial. The normal practice is to list for a prehearing review either before the District Judge or the trial judge. It is common practice for the judge to encourage the parties to agree on how to proceed.

10.8.2   Where the fact is two years separation and consent and consent is withdrawn, the District Judge will stay the proceedings. If this is the only fact relied upon either party may apply to have the petition dismissed.

10.8.3   In a defended suit if it is agreed to proceed on the cross prayer the prayer of the petition should be stayed and permission sought to proceed on the prayer of the cross petition. If the prayer of the petition were dismissed all of the proceedings would cease to subsist.

10.9   DISMISSAL AND TRANSFER

10.9.1   A petition which has not been served may be dismissed without notice. If the petition has been served either party may apply to have it dismissed, the petitioner because he choses to do so and the respondent because the petitioner is not prosecuting the petition.

10.9.2   As there are no limitation periods in matrimonial proceedings the court is usually reluctant to dismiss for want of prosecution where the petitioner demonstrates a willingness to proceed.

10.9.3   A case may be transferred to another divorce county court which includes the Principal Registry. The application is on notice.

10.10   APPLYING FOR DECREE ABSOLUTE

10.10.1   Before applying for decree absolute solicitors should consider whether circumstances exist which make it advisable to delay finalising a decree of divorce until these issues are resolved (for example, outstanding issues relating to pension entitlement, life insurance or inheritance). Solicitors acting for respondents should consider asking petitioners' solicitors to agree in advance that they will not apply on behalf of the petitioner for the decree nisi to be made absolute if this course of action would prejudice respondents or until a financial settlement has been reached between the parties.

10.10.2   Solicitors should also be aware of the procedures available under the Matrimonial Causes Act 1973, s.10(2) to delay the making of a decree absolute in cases brought under s.1(2)(d) and (e) of that Act (relating to two or five years' separation) pending the consideration of the respondent's position.

10.10.3   Solicitors acting for respondents on divorce must discourage their clients from making inappropriate applications for decree absolute and make it clear that an inappropriate application may be penalised in costs.

10.10.4   Clients should be advised that they may be prejudiced, both in terms of law and procedure, if they remarry after decree absolute but before an application for ancillary relief is made on their behalf. Respondent clients should, therefore, be advised in writing not to remarry before an application for ancillary relief has been made.

10.10.5   All clients should be advised that a decree absolute does not bring to an end financial claims between the parties even if there are no assets to be divided.

PART 11

Ancillary relief

11.1 OVERRIDING OBJECTIVE

11.1.1 When conducting an ancillary relief case, regard must always be had to the overriding objective set out at the Family Proceedings Rules (FPR) 1991, rule 2.51B. The procedural rules which govern an application for ancillary relief are set out in FPR 1991 as amended.

11.1.2 Rule 2.51B states that the Rules are a 'procedural code with the overriding objective of enabling the court to deal with cases justly'. This includes ensuring the parties are on equal footing, saving expense, dealing with the case in ways which are proportionate, ensuring that it is dealt with expeditiously and fairly and allocating to it an appropriate share of the court's resources.

11.2 VOLUNTARY DISCLOSURE, NEGOTIATION AND THE PRE-APPLICATION

11.2.1 The extent and format of voluntary disclosure can be agreed between solicitors although reference should be made to the pre-action protocol annexed to *Practice Direction (Ancillary Relief Procedure)* [2000] 1 FLR 997 which provides guidance for the extent and format of voluntary disclosure. The use of a Form E or part of it can be a helpful method of providing disclosure, but excessive or disproportionate costs should be avoided.

11.2.2 Issuing proceedings in order to take advantage of the court's timetable and powers to require disclosure should not be seen as an aggressive step. Frequently, it can focus the parties' minds on a negotiated settlement.

11.3 FINANCIAL APPLICATION

11.3.1 The application is usually in Form A or Form B (application under the Matrimonial Causes Act (MCA) 1973, s.10(2) to consider the financial position of a respondent under a two year or five year separation divorce/dissolution).

11.3.2 The relief sought must be specified. Property adjustment applications require identification of the particular property, registered title number and details of mortgagee. The court will serve on the respondent. Solicitors should serve on pension providers and mortgagees.

11.3.3 If the details of property or pension arrangements are not available when issuing, Form A or Form B should be amended later when the information is known.

11.4 INTERIM ORDERS

Maintenance pending suit and interim periodical payments

11.4.1 MCA 1973, s.22 empowers the court to order periodical payments commencing not earlier than the date of the presentation of the petition and to continue not beyond the pronouncement of the decree absolute. Interim periodical payments are available after the decree absolute and the same principle applies, namely that the court has a wide discretion to make such maintenance provision as it thinks reasonable. It is important for the applicant for maintenance pending suit to ensure that the order goes on to provide for interim periodical payments following decree absolute as otherwise the order will lapse.

11.4.2 These applications are under FPR 1991, rule 2.69F and useful guidance may be found in *TL* v. *ML (Ancillary Relief: Claim against Assets of Extended Family)* [2005] EWHC 2860 (Fam).

11.4.3 MCA 1973, s.23(3)(a) gives the court power to make an order for a capital sum limited to expenses incurred before the date of the application. There has to be a decree nisi and the order is arguably not effective until the decree absolute. These applications are not used very often, but can be useful and should not be ignored. It is to be noted, however, that this is not tantamount to the court having power to make an 'interim lump sum order' on account of the eventual settlement.

11.4.4 MCA 1973, s.27(1) empowers the court to make maintenance and lump sum orders if the respondent has failed to provide reasonable maintenance for the applicant or has failed to provide a proper contribution towards reasonable maintenance for any child of the family. No divorce proceedings are needed for such an application but divorce/dissolution does not preclude such an application within which a lump sum application may be made. Nevertheless, it would be unusual to run both ancillary relief and section 27 proceedings together in view of the duplication of work and costs.

Funding of the fees by court application

11.4.5   A 'costs allowance' to meet the ongoing expense of legal representation can be part of a maintenance pending suit application. In order to be successful the applicant will have to show that:

- there are no assets or none that can reasonably be deployed for costs;
- it is not possible or reasonable to borrow;
- it is not possible or reasonable to defer payment to the legal representatives through a charge on the outcome of the application (a *Sears Tooth* agreement: *Sears Tooth* v. *Payne Hicks Beach* [1997] 2 FLR 116);
- it is not possible to secure public funding at a level of expertise apt to the proceedings;
- a costs allowance is appropriate in view of the nature of the proceedings and the reasonableness of the applicant's approach to those proceedings;
- the respondent has the resources to be able to make the payments sought;
- the applicant's solicitors may not continue to act if the application is refused.

(*A* v. *A (Maintenance Pending Suit: Provision for Legal Fees)* [2001] 1 FLR 377; *Moses-Taiga* v. *Taiga* [2005] EWCA Civ 1013 and *TL* v. *ML* [2005] EWHC 2860 (Fam).)

11.5   DISCLOSURE

Duty of disclosure

11.5.1   The ancillary relief procedure is designed to encourage openness, prevent delay, identify issues and ensure that disclosure is proportionate to the issues and the value of the assets in question.

11.5.2   The duty of disclosure must be considered in accordance with the law, judicial recommended practice, the Solicitors' Code of Conduct 2007, this Family Law Protocol and the Resolution Code of Practice.

11.5.3   Individuals need to be informed of the requirement to be open and honest as failure to do so will reduce trust and make constructive and non-confrontational dialogue more difficult and settlement less possible. Dishonest disclosure may also amount to a criminal offence.

11.5.4   Disclosure relates to facts and documents (see *Practice Direction (Family Proceedings: Case Management)* [1995] 1 FLR 456, 31 January 1995):

> It is a duty owed to the court both by the parties and by their legal representatives to give full and frank disclosure in ancillary relief applications and also in all matters in respect of children..

In *I* v. *I* [2008] EWHC 1167 (Fam) it was said that the duty of full and frank disclosure includes a duty to:

- provide information that would set the other side on a line of enquiry or a thought process on matters to which the court must have regard;
- provide information that may remove uncertainty as to the value of an asset or the amount of future income or inform the assessment of income or values.

If there is any doubt about the effect of a particular piece of information, disclosure should be given.

11.5.5   The failure to disclose may:

- result in inferences of greater assets;
- result in a finding of litigation misconduct and a costs order;
- reduce the credibility of the client.

11.6   PRIVILEGE

11.6.1   The law of privilege is complex and beyond the scope of this chapter. However, as a matter of good practice:

- Facts should not be disclosed in 'without prejudice' correspondence but instead should appear in a separate open letter.
- The *Practice Direction (Ancillary Relief Procedure)* [2000] 1 FLR 997 states that the court expects parties to make offers and proposals and to give them proper consideration at the FDR appointment. The duty to negotiate is conditional upon there having been proper disclosure. The use of privileged communications is to be encouraged to further attempts to settle.
- Evidence of any negotiations or concessions made in the course of an FDR appointment will not be admissible in evidence at the final

hearing. However, it must be noted that no privilege can attach to statements of fact, whether made at an FDR or in 'without prejudice' correspondence.

11.7   SELF-HELP

11.7.1   The Court of Appeal decision in *Tchenguiz* v. *Imerman; Imerman* v. *Imerman* [2010] EWCA Civ 908 has significantly altered the advice to clients in relation to self-help and *Hildebrand* documents ([1992] 1 FLR 244). The practical implications of this 29 July 2010 judgment are being considered and a preliminary view is that:

- It is an actionable breach of confidence to examine, copy, retain or use a confidential document. Confidence exists between spouses.
- *Hildebrand* is only good law for the timing of disclosure of documents.
- There is no legal basis for 'self-help disclosure'.
- A spouse whose documents have been purloined is entitled to an injunction for return of documents, preventing use and destruction of copies.
- The duty of disclosure only arises upon the requirement to file and serve a Form E and then a spouse has remedies of applying to the court for disclosure and injunctions.

11.7.2   The client needs to be advised that self-help may lead to enforcement action outside of family proceedings including:

- Human Rights Act 1998
- Data Protection Act 1998
- Computer Misuse Act 1990
- Regulation of Investigatory Powers Act 2000
- Copyright, Designs and Patents Act 1988
- Postal Services Act 2000
- Civil action in tort/breach of contract.

11.7.3   Practitioners also need to be aware that they could become personally liable or be in breach of the law in certain circumstances.

11.7.4   In appropriate cases clients should be advised of the court's powers to make search and preservation orders together with injunction orders under MCA 1973, s.37.

11.7.5   Clients should be informed that the practical and procedural consequences of self-help may result in:

- increasing tension and hostility;

- encouraging vindictive and/or corresponding action by the other party;
- increased costs;
- children being adversely affected;
- an order for costs;
- reduced prospects of a negotiated settlement.

11.8   EXPERT EVIDENCE

11.8.1   Paragraphs 3.8 and 3.14 of the Pre-Application Protocol annexed to *Practice Direction (Ancillary Relief Procedure)* [2000] FLR 997 and the President's Ancillary Relief Advisory Group *Best Practice Guide for Instructing a Single Joint Expert* must be followed.

11.8.2   Part 35 of the Civil Procedure Rules 1998 (CPR) applies to ancillary relief proceedings.

11.8.3   It is often entirely acceptable to have a broad assessment of the value of an asset. Lawyers should guard against incurring disproportionate costs in pursuing valuations.

11.8.4   Professional witnesses must be made aware of their duty to the court and to avoid a partisan approach.

11.9   FIRST DIRECTIONS APPOINTMENT

11.9.1   In order to ensure that the first directions appointment (FDA) is as productive and as cost effective as possible solicitors should:

- Ensure that the client is aware of his obligation to attend the hearing and that it may last some considerable time.
- Exchange statements of issues, chronologies, questionnaires and Form G 14 days before the date of the first appointment.
- Ensure that questionnaires are drafted by reference to the issues in the case. In more complex cases it can be helpful for each question, or section of questions, to be annotated with specific reference to the relevant issue.
- Discuss the other party's documentation and consider whether any challenges are to be made to the questionnaire.
- Assemble details of experts, their fees and availability so that a decision about whom to instruct can be made at the appointment.
- Consider whether to provide a case outline including a summary of financial resources.

- Consider drafting an order of the directions sought. Note that many courts have their own standard directions to which reference should be made.
- Prepare a costs estimate in Form H. If seeking a costs order in relation to the FDA itself, prepare a schedule for summary assessment. This will be appropriate where, for example, the appointment cannot be effective due to the failure of a party to provide Form E or otherwise comply with the rules.
- If the appointment is to be a combined FDA/FDR hearing prepare as set out below.

11.10   FINANCIAL DISPUTE RESOLUTION HEARING

11.10.1   Before an FDR hearing solicitors should:

- Ensure that the client understands the purpose and format of an FDR hearing, including the issue of privilege.
- Have exchanged offers of settlement prior to the appointment.
- Have discussed with the client what are the non-negotiable aspects of settlement terms.
- Prepare a case outline attaching all offers of settlement so that submissions to the judge can be made by reference to that case outline.
- Make a clear note of how negotiations develop at court and a clear note of the other party's submissions to the judge and the judge's indications.

11.10.2   If an agreement is reached it should be recorded either in the form of heads of agreement or, preferably, in a fully drafted order. In both cases, the parties must read through the order carefully and it should then be signed by the parties themselves and their respective legal advisers. If instructed, counsel should sign.

11.10.3   It is critical to know whether or not an order has been made by the judge if agreement has been reached (a *Rose* order (see **3.7**)). A fully detailed draft is not a pre-requisite to the making of an order. It is possible for the order to be made on the basis of clear heads of agreement, with a view to the order being perfected subsequently. If an order has not been made, then a written agreement can still be a *Xydhias* agreement (see **3.8**), which the client should understand is unlikely easily to be resiled from (*Rose* v. *Rose* [2002] EWCA Civ 208 and *Xydhias* v. *Xydhias* [1999] 2 All ER 386).

11.10.4   If an agreement has not been reached ensure that you have a detailed attendance note prepared, a copy of which should be provided to the client.

11.10.5   If agreement has not been reached, the power of the court is limited to fixing a final hearing, making directions or adjourning the FDR hearing: FPR 1991, rule 2.61E(2) and *Myerson* v. *Myerson* [2008] EWCA Civ 1376.

11.10.6   At the conclusion of the FDR hearing ensure that all FDR outlines and without prejudice letters are removed from the court file.

11.11   PREPARATION FOR THE FINAL HEARING

11.11.1   In respect of the preparation of bundles, *Practice Direction (Family Proceedings: Court Bundles)* [2000] 1 FLR 537 applies to all hearings in the High Court (including the Principal Registry of the Family Division) and all hearings with a time estimate of half a day or more in other courts. The content, presentation and timing of delivery of bundles is set out in the Practice Direction and this should be adhered to to ensure that the hearing takes place efficiently and to avoid criticism of solicitors and possible adverse costs consequences.

11.11.2   Not less than 14 days before the date fixed for the final hearing the applicant's solicitors must file and serve open proposals. Seven days following that the respondent must do likewise.

11.11.3   The advocate will need to provide as part of the bundle:

- case summary;
- statement of issue or issues to be determined;
- summary of the order or directions sought;
- a chronology if a summary is insufficient;
- skeleton arguments with copies of authorities relied upon.

11.11.4   For a final hearing a costs schedule in Form H1 should be prepared. It should be noted that this is a much more complicated document than the Form H prepared for hearings other than a final hearing. Consideration will need to be given to the costs of implementing orders so it is important, for example, to ensure that full details of the cost of pension implementation and property transfers are available.

11.11.5   As soon as a final hearing has been notified it is good practice to note on your case plan and diarise the necessary steps to be taken in the run up to the final hearing. For example, in order to lodge the trial bundle two clear days prior to the hearing it is necessary to provide:

- a date for the preparation of the trial bundle index;

- time provided for the trial bundle index to be considered by the other party;
- time to actually produce the bundle.

In any event the advocate will wish to have the trial bundle well before the hearing in order to prepare the case summary.

11.12   CONSENT ORDERS

11.12.1   When drafting the order solicitors should:

- Use precedents. Resolution's precedents for consent orders are universally used and accepted, having been approved by the judiciary.
- Recognise the limits of the court's powers and where the agreement includes provisions which the court cannot order, include those as undertakings/declarations/recitals/agreements.
- Check local practice as to who has to sign the consent order particularly if undertakings are being provided and also whether a Form A 'for dismissal purposes only' is required.
- Where a pension sharing or attachment order is to be made, ensure that notice has been given to the provider and that the required pension sharing annex has been completed correctly, including details of how any costs of the pension sharing/attachment are to be met.

Statement of information

11.12.2   Where an order is being made by consent in circumstances where the parties are not actually at court, under FPR 1991, rule 2.61 a statement of each party's financial and personal circumstances needs to be completed unless dispensed with by the judge. To avoid delay or rejection it is essential not only to provide full information but to present the financial circumstances in such a way that the judge can easily understand how both parties are to be left as a result of the implementation of the agreed terms. A schedule showing the net effect of the agreement is an effective way of achieving such an objective. The notes section in the statement can also be used to good effect in explaining the position.

11.12.3   A consent order for maintenance pending suit and variation of maintenance requires more limited information, but practice varies and certainly if the consent order capitalises maintenance full information is normally required.

11.13 COSTS

Definition of 'ancillary relief'

11.13.1 'Ancillary relief' is defined by FPR 1991, rule 1.2 as:

- an avoidance of disposition order under MCA 1973;
- a financial provision order under MCA 1973, s.21(1) except an order under s.27(6);
- an order for maintenance pending suit;
- a property adjustment order;
- a variation order;
- a pension sharing order.

11.13.2 The above are governed by the Family Proceedings (Amendment) Rules 2006, SI 2006/352, 'the New Rules' which inserted a new rule 2.71 'costs orders' into FPR 1991.

11.13.3 Rule 2.71(4)(a) provides 'the general rule in ancillary relief proceedings is that the court will not make an order requiring one party to pay the costs of another party', but under rule 2.71(4)(b):

> the court may make such an order at any stage of the proceedings where it considers it appropriate to do so because of the conduct of the party in relation to the proceedings (whether before or during them).

Factors the court must take into account

11.13.4 Having established the general rule of no order for costs, rule 2.71(5) lists the factors which the court must take into account in deciding what order, if any, to make under rule 2.71(4)(b).

11.13.5 The rule 2.71(5) factors are:

- any failure to comply with the rules, any order of the court or any practice directions which the court considers relevant;
- any open offer to settle;
- whether it is reasonable for a party to raise, pursue or contest a particular allegation or issue;
- the manner in which the party has pursued or responded to the application or a particular allegation or issue;
- any other aspect of the parties' conduct in relation to the proceedings which the court considers relevant; and
- the financial effect on the parties of any costs order.

Application for a costs order

11.13.6 If you intend to make an application for a costs order this should be made plain in open correspondence or in skeleton arguments prior to the hearing. If a summary assessment of costs would be appropriate it is necessary to file a statement of costs in CPR Form N260.

11.13.7 Some practical considerations are:

- Costs will be argued during the hearing rather than after judgement. Costs arguments, therefore, need to be marshalled and prepared and then reconsidered as evidence is given during the hearing.
- Directions may be needed concerning costs issues identifying the issues and the costs attributable to these particular issues.
- Sophisticated costs breakdowns will be required to identify the additional costs incurred because of, for example, one party pursuing a particular issue.
- It is quite likely that an indication of making a costs application will result in a cross application.
- The judge's attitude to particular issues during the hearing may well influence costs arguments.
- The solicitor may need to explain how a particular aspect of the case has been conducted. This may place the solicitor in a difficult position because the client may have insisted upon pursuing a particular line of enquiry contrary to solicitor's advice.
- Issues about costs may influence who is present in court during the hearing: an agent or a trainee may be inappropriate and inadequate.
- A last minute Form H will not be acceptable. A detailed costs breakdown over particular periods may well be needed.

Offers

11.13.8 The new rules mark the end of '*Calderbank*' offers because the judge will not see these offers. The trial judge will only consider open offers.

11.13.9 Rule 2.67(6) of FPR 1991 states that 'no offer to settle which is not an open offer to settle shall be admissible at any stage of the proceedings except as provided by Rule 2.61E (the FDR appointment)'.

11.13.10 Practice varies around the country but it is believed that there are relatively few open offers made during the course of an application and often only one offer made sometimes even less than the 14 days required prior to the hearing date.

11.13.11   Without prejudice offers (as opposed to *Calderbank* offers) still have their place in proceedings. Although these cannot be seen by the court, and therefore have no relevance to the issue of costs, they can still be an important factor in negotiations.

11.14   CIVIL PARTNERSHIPS

11.14.1   The Civil Partnership Act 2004, s.72(1) states that Sched.5 (which contains ancillary relief provisions) corresponds to provision for financial relief in marriages.

11.14.2   Schedule 5 lists relief available and resembles MCA 1973. Paragraph 21(2) lists the factors to consider which mirror MCA 1973, s.25.

11.14.3   Maintenance pending the outcome of proceedings is available.

11.14.4   An application for failure to provide reasonable maintenance is available whether or not there are dissolution proceedings.

11.14.5   A periodical payments order terminates after whichever comes first of death or the civil partnership or marriage of the recipient of the periodical payments.

PART 12

Cohabitation

Solicitors should keep under review at all times the availability of public funding and the need to provide clients with costs information at the outset and on a regular basis.

12.1   SCOPE

12.1.1   English law does not yet recognise cohabitation as a defined legal status and so very few specific rights exist for cohabitants. This position is becoming untenable as increasing numbers of the population (1 in 6 of all couples according to the 2001 census) live together without marrying or, if same-sex, entering into a civil partnership. The problems they face on relationship breakdown are similar to those faced by couples who have married or who are civil partners.

12.1.2   The lack of a single statute to deal with cohabitants can make the task of resolving their problems particularly complex. The Law Commission has acknowledged this and proposed reform of this area of law in 2007 (*Cohabitation: The Financial Consequences of Relationship Breakdown* (Cm 7182)). However, the government announced that it would postpone action until it had studied research findings following the implementation of the earlier Family Law (Scotland) Act 2006, which had introduced some specific remedies for cohabitants in that jurisdiction, and so failed to support Lord Lester's Cohabitation Bill in the House of Lords in 2009. Meanwhile, a bill has been introduced in Eire which would, inter alia, have the effect of introducing similar remedies for cohabitants in that country (the Civil Partnership Bill 2009). There are, of course, remedies for cohabitants in many other jurisdictions. Solicitors should be alert to prospective changes to the law and the need to advise clients accordingly.

12.1.3   Much of the Protocol applies equally to cohabiting couples as to married couples or civil partners. See in particular, the approach contained in the Main Protocol (see **Part 1**) and also **Parts 5** and **6** (relating to children), **Part 4** (domestic abuse) and **Part 2** (mediation/alternative dispute resolution).

12.1.4 It is primarily in the area of finances that the options available to cohabit-ants on relationship breakdown differ greatly from those available to spouses or civil partners. This section of the Protocol deals mainly with those financial claims which arise on cohabitation breakdown. The key point for solicitors to remember in this area is that there is usually no discretion for the court to adjust the interests of the parties in order to achieve a fair outcome. The most that the court can do is to declare and enforce their existing interests, applying established principles of trust and property law.

12.1.5 Solicitors must be aware that same-sex couples who register their relation-ship under the Civil Partnership Act 2004 acquire rights equivalent to those of married couples and should not be treated as cohabitants.

12.1.6 Solicitors should bear in mind that it may occasionally be necessary to ascertain the beneficial interests in property in the case of even a married couple or civil partners where there is a third-party claim against the interest of one of them, e.g. following bankruptcy or the making of a charging order, and that in such circumstances the procedure outlined in **12.4–12.5** would apply.

12.2 ADVICE AT THE COMMENCEMENT OF OR DURING COHABITATION

12.2.1 Experience shows that most clients are completely unaware of their legal position when they cohabit and that they usually have misconceptions as to their rights. Clients may consult solicitors either at the start of their relationship or during it and solicitors should use such opportunities to explain to clients their legal position.

12.2.2 Clients may seek advice at the commencement of a relationship. If so, they should be encouraged to consider entering into a formal cohabitation agreement, if such an agreement would be beneficial to them. Solicitors should have access to appropriate precedents for cohabitation agreements at all times (model cohabitation agreements can be obtained from Resolu-tion and from a number of other sources (see **Appendix A**)). Solicitors must advise clients that they can only act for one of the parties in drawing up such an agreement and that the other party must be separately represented.

12.2.3 Clients should be referred to the Advice Now website (see **www.advicenow.org.uk/living-together**) which is funded by the Ministry of Justice as part of its Living Together campaign. They may also wish to consider the 'Living Together Agreement' which is published on that website.

12.2.4   Clients will often consult solicitors when they are intending to purchase a property together. In such circumstances, careful consideration needs to be given as to how the property is to be held. Particular care is needed where the property is to be held in the name of only one of them or where they have made or are intending to make unequal contributions towards the purchase price. If legal title is to be held in their joint names, solicitors must discuss with them the implications of owning the property either as beneficial joint tenants or tenants in common and ascertain whether a declaration of trust is desirable and/or whether they wish to enter into a cohabitation agreement. To fail to give and record such advice in an appropriate case can lead to a claim for negligence.

12.2.5   Where cohabitants decide to prepare a declaration of trust at the time of purchase of a property, solicitors can act for both cohabitants in preparing the declaration only if it is clear that there is complete agreement from the outset as to all the terms of the declaration and there is no conflict of interest.

12.2.6   At all relevant times, solicitors should advise cohabitants about the importance of making wills, making pension and death-in-service benefit nominations, considering life assurance policies and the benefits of parental responsibility agreements. Solicitors should also advise as to what might occur in the event that these matters are not dealt with. Such advice should be recorded in writing.

12.2.7   Cohabitants should be warned that there is no equivalent to the spouse exemption for them on inheritance tax (IHT) and therefore that gifts made within seven years of death will attract IHT. At the time of the making of a will, estate planning should be discussed. Practitioners should advise clients of the effect of the ruling in *Holland* v. *IRC* [2003] WTLR 207 which confirmed that the lack of spouse exemption from IHT for cohabitants is not in breach of the Human Rights Act 1998. Unless there is a change in the law there will be no tax relief on any gifts between cohabitants other than in the normal way. Note that since the Civil Partnership Act 2004, there has been a tax exemption for registered civil partners equivalent to the spouse exemption for married couples.

12.2.8   Solicitors are reminded that they may need to liaise with conveyancing practitioners or third parties who are involved in any existing wills, trusts or settlements. They should obtain letters of authority from their client where appropriate. Solicitors must avoid giving investment advice unless authorised to do so.

12.3 ADVICE FOLLOWING RELATIONSHIP BREAKDOWN

12.3.1 At the first meeting or early on in the case, solicitors should consider and advise, where appropriate, on all the matters referred to in **Part 1**. The sections relating to reconciliation and other support services apply equally to cohabitation.

12.3.2 The paragraphs relating to family dispute resolution, mediation and collaborative law in **Part 2** are also equally applicable in cohabitation cases. Accordingly, solicitors must, at an early stage, unless it is clearly inappropriate to do so, explain the mediation process and advise clients on the benefits and/or limitations of mediation and/or collaborative law in their particular case as well as the role of solicitors in supporting the mediation process. The suitability of mediation should be kept under review throughout the case and clients should be referred to mediation when and where appropriate.

12.3.3 The rest of **Part 1** will apply equally to cohabitation cases and should be referred to. It is important that solicitors screen appropriately for domestic abuse and consider whether there are any urgent issues to be dealt with.

12.3.4 Solicitors should check whether a client has made a will and, if so, consider with them whether it is still appropriate in the circumstances.

12.3.5 Solicitors should check how the property is held by obtaining office copies of the Land Registry title documentation. They should also consider obtaining a copy of the original conveyancing file relating to the property in question if, for example, there is likely to be any dispute as to original contributions or intentions at the date of purchase.

12.3.6 If the property is held as a joint tenancy, then consideration should be given to severing the joint tenancy and an appropriate notice prepared, signed by the client and served on the other property owner.

12.3.7 Solicitors should consider whether it is necessary to register a restriction at the Land Registry to protect a client's interest in a property. This is done by completion of Form RX1 with a request for entry of a standard-form restriction, usually in Form A of Sched.4 to the Land Registration Rules 2003, SI 2003/1417. Reference may be had to Land Registry Practice Guide 24: Private Trusts of Land (2009) (at **www.landregistry.gov.uk**). Provided that the application is clearly worded and shows how and why the client's beneficial interest arose, this will be accepted by the Land Registry as evidence that the client has 'sufficient interest'. It should be noted that the Land Registry will give the (other) registered owner of the land notice of the application and an opportunity to object. If a dispute is identified at this stage, the matter may be referred to the Land Registry Adjudicator for determination, although in practice the adjudicator will usually direct one or other of the parties to commence court proceedings within a specified time-frame.

12.3.8   Solicitors should consider whether to advise a client to contact the mortgage company to place a dispute indicator on their records in order to prevent one party from drawing down on the mortgage if there is any flexibility to do so.

12.3.9   In certain cases it may be appropriate to write and request that the other side consent to the mortgage being converted to interest-only whilst the issues are sorted out, or if one person is paying a lot more, write and put them on notice that they may expect credit by way of equitable accounting. For example, an application under the Children Act (CA) 1989, Sched.1 would not provide for anything other than an interest-only mortgage, but if the father is meeting the mortgage on a repayment basis he is in effect adding to the mother's capital which is not permitted by Sched.1.

12.3.10   Matters relating to children and the provision of information are equally applicable to cohabitation cases, although it is acknowledged that the availability of standard information for cohabitants is not as wide as for other family matters.

12.3.11   Under **1.5** of **Part 1** it is important that solicitors should, at the end of the first meeting or at an early stage, outline the possible remedies that are available and the possible outcomes, as far as this is practical with the information available. It is important that clients are not given unrealistic expectations either of what can be achieved or of the time the matter may take to resolve.

12.3.12   Solicitors should advise clients that they might have claims in both property law and family law. Property law claims may be claims for a beneficial interest in a property by way of a resulting or constructive trust dealt with under the Trusts of Land and Appointment of Trustees Act (TLATA) 1996, or proprietary estoppel and/or equitable accounting. If a couple has children, a client may also have claims under CA 1989, Sched.1 and the Child Support Act 1991 (as amended). In exceptional cases these can extend effectively to support of the parent as well as the child.

12.3.13   Solicitors need to bear in mind that practice and procedure for property law and family law claims are very different, the former being governed by the Civil Procedure Rules 1998 (CPR) as amended, the latter by the Family Proceedings Rules (FPR) 1991, SI 1991/1247 and the Family Procedings Courts (Children Act 1989) Rules (FPCR) 1991, SI 1991/1395 as amended.

This is a developing area of law (see for example the cases of *Stack* v. *Dowden* [2007] UKHL 17 and *Kernott* v. *Jones* [2010] EWCA Civ 578) and solicitors must ensure that they are aware of the latest case law and confident in their knowledge before offering advice in this area.

12.3.14　When dealing with property claims of cohabiting couples, solicitors should also check to see if they were engaged. Provided that less than three years has elapsed since any engagement was broken off, an application could also be made under the Married Women's Property Act (MWPA) 1882 for a declaration in respect of property (which would include chattels).

12.3.15　Although in general, engaged couples are treated in the same way as unmarried couples, solicitors should be aware of the Law Reform (Miscellaneous Provisions) Act (LR(MP)A) 1970, s.3(1) relating to gifts between engaged couples and also the Matrimonial Proceedings and Property Act (MPPA) 1970, s.37 allowing an entitled applicant to argue that he has a share, or an increased share, in property by virtue of substantial contributions to the improvement of that property. In practice, MPPA 1970, s.37 is rarely relied upon because such works would usually now form the basis of a constructive trust or proprietary estoppel claim. They would, however, be family proceedings and FPR 1991 would apply.

12.3.16　There are similar provisions relating to those who were in an agreement to enter into a civil partnership which has been terminated within the last three years (Civil Partnership Act 2004, s.74) – see s.65 for the equivalent to MPPA 1970, s.37; s.66 for MWPA 1882; and s.74(5) for LR(MP)A 1970.

12.3.17　The above provisions are particularly useful in relation to property other than real property. Claims concerning real property are better dealt with under the TLATA 1996 as the court has a wider discretion and can, for example, delay sale.

12.3.18　Requirements for solicitors to provide costs information as outlined in the Main Protocol (see **1.8**) apply equally to cohabitation cases. Clients should be advised realistically as to likely costs and solicitors should be aware that contested applications are significantly more expensive than, for example, comparable ancillary relief proceedings. In addition, significant civil court fees are payable on issue, on allocation, on listing and for trial.

12.3.19　Public funding may be available where the proceedings relate to the ownership or possession of the client's home (*Legal Services Commission Manual*, para.3C-014). Applications under TLATA 1996 are not 'family proceedings' within the meaning of the Courts and Legal Services Act 1990 and so they can be funded under a conditional fee agreement. If so, an appropriate funding notice must be served on the other party as any success fee would otherwise be unrecoverable under CPR, rule 44.3B(1)(c).

12.3.20   Clients should be advised that, unlike most other 'family' proceedings, the court is likely to make a costs order in favour of whichever party is considered to have 'won' the case – since under CPR, rule 44.3(2)(a) the general rule is that costs will follow the event.

12.3.21   The provisions within the Main Protocol as to communications with the other party (see **1.9**) and the giving of notice of issue of proceedings (see **1.11**) are both applicable to cohabitation cases.

12.3.22   Clients should be reminded at this early stage that cohabitation cases depend heavily on evidence. Consideration should be given as to how the case is to be pleaded and the evidence that will be necessary in order to prove that case. Witness statements should be taken from the client and any likely witnesses and clients should be advised of the necessity of keeping and producing relevant documentary evidence (e.g. bank statements, receipts and the like) as the case proceeds. Solicitors should seek to establish the strength of the client's case at this early stage and advise appropriately.

12.4   PRIOR TO ISSUING PROCEEDINGS FOR FINANCIAL MATTERS

Voluntary disclosure and ADR

12.4.1   Solicitors must consider and discuss the following with clients:

1.   The importance of pre-application disclosure and negotiation. An application must not be issued when settlement is a reasonable prospect. Solicitors are referred to the *Pre-Application Protocol for Ancillary Relief* (see **11.5**). Making an application to the court should not be regarded as a hostile step or a last resort but rather as a way of starting the court timetable, controlling disclosure and endeavouring to avoid the cost of final hearing.

2.   The most appropriate form of dispute resolution for the case, based on clients' needs and individual circumstances, at an early stage. Solicitors must discuss alternative dispute resolution (ADR) with clients, except where it is inappropriate to do so, and advise on whether it is likely to be suitable to their case and, where appropriate, refer them to an appropriate individual (see **Part 2**).

Identifying the issues

12.4.2   Solicitors must seek to clarify the parties' claims and identify the issues between them as soon as possible. To achieve this the parties must provide, as soon as possible, a full, frank and clear disclosure of facts, information and documents which are material and sufficiently accurate to enable proper negotiations to take place in order to settle their differences. Openness in all dealings is essential.

Pre-action protocol

Civil Procedure Rules 1998

12.4.3   Although there is no protocol specific to TLATA 1996 cases, solicitors (or parties where unrepresented) will be expected to comply with Annex A of the *Practice Direction (Pre-Action Conduct)* which applies to all types of civil cases and therefore to cohabitants in proceedings under TLATA 1996.

12.4.4   The common objectives of all the pre-action protocols are as follows:

- to encourage the early and full exchange of information between the parties about any dispute between them which might need resolution by a court;
- to enable the parties to avoid proceedings by agreeing a settlement of the claim before commencement of proceedings, either through negotiation directly between them, with or without the assistance of a mediator if appropriate, or negotiation between the solicitors; and
- to support the efficient management of proceedings where litigation cannot be avoided.

12.4.5   Under para.4.2 of the Practice Direction, the court will expect the parties and their legal advisers to act reasonably in exchanging information and documents relevant to the claim and generally in trying to avoid the necessity for the commencement of proceedings (in accordance with the overriding objective and the matters referred to in CPR, rule 1.1(2)). In view of the nature of family proceedings, the parties and their representatives should act in a conciliatory and constructive manner at all times.

Pre-action procedure for Trusts of Land and Appointment of Trustees Act 1996 claims

12.4.6   For TLATA 1996 claims, solicitors (or unrepresented parties) should comply with the following key elements of pre-action procedure, if appropriate, unless there are very good reasons for not doing so. They should:

141

1. Send an initial letter (referred to in the CPR as a 'letter of claim') setting out the following information in concise form:

   (a) a clear summary of uncontroversial facts;

   (b) the main allegations of fact, including where appropriate a summary of what was said by the parties at the time;

   (c) an indication of the exact financial claim;

   (d) indications as to witnesses and a summary of their evidence;

   (e) disclosure of any relevant documents supporting the claim.

   Care should be exercised to ensure that the tone of the letter is non-threatening and sets out facts in a non-aggressive way. If addressed to a party who is not represented the letter must advise the party to seek legal advice and should enclose a second copy of the letter to facilitate this.

2. If possible and appropriate, refrain from issuing proceedings for six weeks, during which time full disclosure should be given and negotiations commenced.

3. If responding, give a preliminary reply within two weeks of receiving the initial letter of claim.

4. If responding, give a full reply within four weeks of receiving the letter of claim.

12.4.7 Preparation of the initial letter of claim will involve a substantial financial commitment from clients. Solicitors must give proper advice to ensure that the claim is framed in the correct way bearing in mind that the court will impose penalties if the case is later presented on a different basis.

12.4.8 Solicitors must consider and discuss with clients the fact that failure to comply with the pre-action protocol may lead to an order for indemnity costs and other financial penalties. CPR, rule 43.3(5)(a) requires the court to consider the conduct of the parties before, as well as during, the proceedings and in particular the extent to which the party has followed the relevant protocol. If no letter is sent, then this will usually be regarded as unreasonable conduct and indemnity costs will be awarded against the claimant.

12.4.9 Solicitors must consider with clients whether the immediate issue of proceedings is required in order to obtain protection of assets. An injunction can be sought to restrain the disposal of an asset pending final hearing. Reference should be made to CPR, Part 25.

12.4.10 If matters between the parties are concluded without the issue of court proceedings, the outcome should be recorded in a formal deed.

12.5   ISSUE AND CONDUCT OF PROCEEDINGS

12.5.1   Applications for an order under TLATA 1996, s.14 (usually brought under CPR, Part 8) will be issued on Form N208 with a claim form, a signed statement of truth and a witness statement from the claimant. They attract a court issue fee. The defendant has 14 days from receipt of the claim in which to file an acknowledgement of service and witness statement. In practice, 14 days will seldom be long enough and it would be usual to agree a voluntary extension.

12.5.2   Solicitors will be aware that the proceedings will offer only a declaration of an equitable interest in a property and a consequential order, for example an order for sale.

12.5.3   Solicitors should note that if there is to be a substantial question of fact or law raised within a case, e.g. a dispute as to whether a claimant has any beneficial interest in the property at all or as to the extent of that interest, it will be more appropriate to issue the proceedings under the CPR, Part 7 procedure with a claim in Form N201 supported by formal particulars of claim containing full details of the legal basis of the claim and remedies sought. Although a strict reading of CPR, rule 64.3 and PD 64A, para.1(1)(a)(iii) suggests that Part 8 should be used for these applications, the court is unlikely in practice to raise any issue if the Part 7 procedure is used, particularly if the parties have agreed to its use. Claims commenced under Part 8 can be transferred to Part 7 at an early stage under CPR, rule 8.8 if the other party objects, or by the court itself under rule 8.1(3).

12.5.4   It should be noted that there are specific requirements for the contents of particulars of claim and reference should be made to CPR, rule 16.4 and para.7 of the accompanying Practice Direction.

12.5.5   In all cases, further consideration should be given to mediation as the court will agree to stay the proceedings for a fixed period to enable the parties to attempt to settle the action either by negotiation or another form of ADR.

12.5.6   Most applications under Part 7 will be allocated to the multi-track because they have a value of over £25,000 and/or the court considers that the trial will probably last longer than one day, as will usually be the case. Applications under Part 8 are automatically treated as allocated to the multi-track, although a specific allocation is usually sought if the parties wish to ensure that the route of appeal is to the Court of Appeal (which is not available if the case is merely 'treated as' allocated to that track).

12.5.7   Solicitors should be aware that most interlocutory hearings in civil cases take the form of a telephone hearing, and that it is usually the responsibility of the applicant/claimant to arrange these. BT Legal Conferencing can be contacted on 0800 028 4194 in order to arrange such a hearing.

12.5.8   Although FPR 1991 do not apply to these claims, many courts are prepared to direct that a case management conference be conducted as if it were a financial dispute resolution (FDR) appointment in an ancillary relief application and an appropriate direction should be sought at allocation stage.

12.6   DIRECTIONS

12.6.1   Directions which the court might be asked to make are:

- that the case be listed for a directions appointment for the purpose of assessing the parties' positions and for the purpose of discussion and negotiation;
- that the parties serve signed witness statements in advance;
- that the parties file:
    - details of all offers;
    - a position statement;
    - an agreed statement of issues;
- that the parties shall attend personally;
- that the appointment shall be conducted on a without prejudice basis;
- in the event that the proceedings are not settled at the hearing the district judge hearing the appointment should not make any orders or directions that the case shall be listed for a case management conference.

12.6.2   Note that the court should be asked to list the appointment with a realistic time estimate (at least one hour) and the parties asked to attend one hour prior to narrow the issues.

12.6.3   Clients should be encouraged to make a reasonable offer of settlement and in most cases the procedure under CPR, Part 36 should be followed. The recipient has 21 days in which to accept the offer. If the claimant fails to beat a Part 36 offer, then there are costs consequences.

12.6.4   Clients should be reminded that the trial of an application under TLATA 1996 takes place in open court, to which the public are admitted. Advocates will usually be robed.

12.6.5   Solicitors are advised to carefully consider the provisions of the CPR when undertaking an application under TLATA 1996, and if they feel that they are not sufficiently proficient in this area, should consider taking advice from a more experienced civil practitioner or transferring the file to another solicitor. Failure to comply with the CPR can lead to sanctions, including the automatic striking out of claims or defences at very short notice, if procedural steps are not taken in a timely fashion.

12.7 CLAIMS UNDER THE INHERITANCE (PROVISION FOR FAMILY AND DEPENDANTS) ACT 1975

12.7.1 Most firms distinguish between contentious probate work and claims under the Inheritance (Provision for Family and Dependants) Act (I(PFD)A) 1975. In some firms, I(PFD)A 1975 cases are dealt with by family lawyers.

12.7.2 Solicitors should not undertake without supervision any work which they know to be outside their area of expertise.

12.7.3 If a case appears complex or beyond the expertise of a practitioner they should consider whether the case should be passed to a member of the Association of Contentious Trust and Probate Specialists (ACTAPS). Solicitors are referred to the ACTAPS Practice Guidance Notes and Code of Conduct which can be found on the Association's website at **www.ac-taps.com**. Best practice pre-action procedures are contained in their Draft Pre-Action Protocol for the Resolution of Probate and Trust Disputes and failure to follow this Protocol can lead to costs penalties.

12.7.4 Solicitors must understand that claims brought under I(PFD)A 1975 are also governed by the CPR. In particular, CPR, rule 57.16 clearly requires that claims under I(PFD)A, s.1 be issued under CPR, Part 8, even though the Part 8 procedure is probably not appropriate if there are substantial disputed facts and the case is likely to be dealt with under Part 7.

12.7.5 Particular care needs to be taken as to the persons who are to be parties to the proceedings as it would be usual to have the personal representatives and the beneficiaries of the estate as separate defendants. Solicitors should note that personal representatives have no power to compromise a claim under the I(PFD)A 1975 unless the beneficiaries instruct them to settle the claim. Note also that if any beneficiary is a minor, then the approval of the court will be needed for any settlement.

12.7.6 Solicitors must note that the time limit for issuing a claim is six months from the date of the issue of the grant of representation, for example the date of the grant of probate.

12.7.7   In the case of *Re Parnall (Deceased)* [2003] All ER (D) 40 the court confirmed that it was not appropriate in I(PFD)A 1975 cases to seek to prevent a grant from being issued while negotiating a claim by entering caveat.

12.7.8   Instead, to be put on notice of the issuing of a grant in an estate a request should be made to the Probate Registry for a standing search. The fee is currently £5.00 and covers a period of six months. Successive periods can be covered by making additional applications. If in that period a grant is issued the Registry will send notification of the person who has extracted the grant and solicitors can obtain a copy of the grant. It will therefore be possible to issue a claim within the time limits of the grant.

12.7.9   In view of the time limit for issuing a claim, pre-issue negotiation is necessarily limited, but this may serve to focus the minds of those involved.

12.7.10   It is helpful to agree, wherever possible, that a directions hearing in an I(PFD)A 1975 case be treated similarly to an FDR hearing so that the judge gives an indication of his or her view of a case and an indication to the parties of the costs implications of continuing to a final hearing.

12.7.11   Solicitors requiring information on the subject of probate are referred to the *Probate Practitioner's Handbook* (6th edn, Law Society, 2010) which deals with both contentious probate and I(PFD)A 1975 claims.

12.7.12   Solicitors are reminded that the same civil costs rules apply to claims under I(PFD)A 1975 as to those under TLATA 1996.

12.8   FINANCIAL ISSUES RELATING TO CHILDREN

12.8.1   Solicitors are referred to **Part 5** for guidance on acting in private children law cases, **Part 9** for claims under CA 1989, Sched.1 and **Part 8** for general child support issues (i.e. the Child Maintenance and Enforcement Commission (CMEC)).

12.9   JURISDICTION AND IN WHICH COURT TO COMMENCE PROCEEDINGS

12.9.1   Before proceedings relating to disputes about property, money, other belongings and children are issued, solicitors must consider carefully where they should issue the application. Where proceedings about different issues are being conducted in relation to the same couple, all proceedings must, where possible, be heard in the same court. If there are applications under TLATA 1996 and under CA 1989 they should be consolidated and heard together (*W* v. *W (Joinder of Trusts of Land Act and Children Act Applications)* [2004] 2 FLR 321).

12.9.2   The county court has unlimited jurisdiction under TLATA 1996 although the application must be issued in the appropriate court for the area in which the defendant resides or in which the property is situated. The Principal Registry of the Family Division, which sits as a county court, has full jurisdiction to deal with applications under TLATA 1996, s.14 and such claims can be issued out of the Principal Registry (see CPR, PD 2B, para.3.2 and *Practice Direction (Family Division: Allocation of Cases: Costs)* [1999] 3 All ER 192).

12.9.3   Claims can be issued out of any District Registry of the High Court. Solicitors should be aware that proceedings may not be started in the High Court unless the value of the claim is more than £25,000 (CPR, PD 7A, para.2.1). Subject to that limitation, if the financial value of the claim, the amount in dispute and/or the complexity of the facts, legal issues, remedies or procedures involved and/or the importance of the outcome of the claim to the public in general are such that solicitors believe that the claim ought to be dealt with by a High Court judge, then the case should be issued in the High Court. In any event, a claim with a value of less than £50,000 will generally be transferred to the county court (CPR, PD 29, para.2.2).

12.9.4   Claims may be issued in either the Family Division or Chancery. The Family Division is likely to be the more appropriate where the parties were living together as a family unit, particularly if they have children or if there are to be linked family claims. The latter may be more appropriate if their relationship was more business-like.

APPENDIX A

Useful guidance and online resources

Many of the resources in this book are available to buy or can be downloaded online. Below is a list of relevant organisations and their websites.

PUBLICATIONS, LEAFLETS AND ONLINE GUIDANCE

Advice Now (www.advicenow.org.uk)

Living Together campaign website provides information on the following topics:

- Introduction
- Moving in
- Housing
- Children
- Money and benefits
- Wills and inheriting
- Inheritance tax
- Pensions
- Breaking up
- Next of kin

Cafcass (www.cafcass.gov.uk)

Family Division: Liaison Between Courts in England and Wales and British Embassies and High Commissions Abroad (28 November 2003, reproduced in Appendix 2 of *Enquiries Abroad/Overseas Travel Policy*?
Parenting Plans: Putting your Children First – A Guide for Separating Parents (March 2010)
Representation of Children in Private Law Proceedings (April 2004)
Time for Children (January 2010)

Child Poverty Action Group (www.cpag.org.uk)

Child Support Handbook 2010/11 (CPAG, 2010)
Child Support: The Legislation, Edward Jacobs (CPAG, 2010)

Crown Prosecution Service (www.cps.gov.uk)

Code for Crown Prosecutors (February 2010)
Safeguarding Children: Guidance on Children as Victims and Witnesses (November 2009)

Department for Education (www.education.gov.uk)

Children Act 1989, Guidance and Regulations, volume 1 (revised April 2010)
Special Guardianship Guidance (August 2005)
Working Together to Safeguard Children (March 2010)

Department of Health (www.dh.gov.uk)

LAC 99(29) *Care Plans and Care Proceedings under the Children Act 1989* (August 1999)
Framework for the Assessment of Children in Need and their Families (April 2000)

Law Society (www.lawsociety.org.uk)

Practice Notes

Acting in the absence of a children's guardian (August 2009)
Client care letters (September 2010)

Accreditation schemes

Children Panel
Family Law
Family Mediation

Books (www.lawsociety.org.uk/bookshop)

Ancillary Relief, Andrew Newbury, Shona Alexander and Ann Corrigan (2009)
Child Contact, Miranda Fisher and Sarah Whitten with Noel Arnold (2006)
Civil Partnership, Andrea Woelke (2006)
Domestic Abuse, Jane Wilson (2010)
Good Practice in Child Care Cases (2nd edn), Law Society (2010)
Pensions and Family Breakdown (2nd edn), David Davidson (2008)
Related Family and Criminal Proceedings, General Editor: Ananda Hall (2007)
Resolution Family Law Handbook (2nd edn), General Editor: Andrew Greensmith (2010)
Resolution Family Disputes Handbook, General Editor: Andrew Greensmith (2010)
Tax and Family Breakdown, Jason Lane (2010)

Ministry of Justice (www.justice.gov.uk)

Preparing for Care and Supervision Proceedings (2009)
Protocol for Judicial Case Management in Public Law Children Act Cases (2003)

National Association of Child Contact Centres (www.naccc.org.uk)

Revised Protocol for Referrals of Families to Supported Child Contact Centres by Judges and Magistrates (2010)

Resolution (www.resolution.org.uk)

Claims under Schedule 1 to the Children Act 1989 (2009)
Domestic Abuse Screening Toolkit (2010)
Guide to Good Practice on Service (2009)

Precedents for Consent Orders (2009)
Resolution Code of Practice (2007)
Separation, Pre-marriage and Pre-Civil Partnerships Agreements (2008)

Solicitors Regulation Authority (www.sra.org.uk)

Solicitors' Code of Conduct 2007 (as revised online)

STATUTORY MATERIALS

(see **www.legislation.gov.uk** and Tables of Statutes and Statutory Instruments)

PRACTICE DIRECTIONS AND PRACTICE NOTES

(see **www.hmcourts-service.gov.uk** and **www.justice.gov.uk**)

Practice Direction (Ancillary Relief Procedure) [2000] 1 FLR 997
Practice Direction (Attendance of Media Representatives at Hearings in Family Proceedings)
    [2009] 2 FLR 167
Practice Direction (Children: Removal from the Jurisdiction) [1986] 2 FLR 89
Practice Direction (Experts in Family Proceedings Relating to Children) [2009] 2 FLR 1383
Practice Direction (Family Division: Allocation of Cases: Costs) [1999] 3 All ER 192
Practice Direction (Family Proceedings: Case Management) [1995] 1 FLR 456
Practice Direction (Family Proceedings: Court Bundles) (Universal Practice to be Applied in
    all Courts other than the Family Proceedings Court) [2006] 2 FLR 199
Practice Direction (Family Proceedings: Experts) [2009] 2 FLR 1383
Practice Direction (Family Proceedings: Media Representatives: Applications) [2009] 2 FLR
    167
Practice Direction (Family Proceedings: Media Representatives: Magistrates' Courts) [2009] 2
    FLR 157
Practice Direction (Pre-Action Conduct) (April 2009)
Practice Direction (Public Law Proceedings) (Guide to Case Management) (commonly known
    as the **Public Law Outline**), April 2010
Practice Direction (Representation of Children in Family Proceedings) [2004] 1 FLR 1188
Practice Direction (Residence and Contact Orders – Domestic Violence and Harm) [2009] 2
    FLR 1400
Practice Direction (Revised Private Law Programme) [2010] 2 FLR 717
Practice Note (Cafcass: Representation of Children in Family Proceedings) [2004] 1 FLR 1190
Practice Note (The Official Solicitor: Appointment in Family Proceedings) [2001] 2 FLR 155

OTHER GUIDANCE

Reports

Children Act Sub-Committee of the Lord Chancellor's Advisory Board on Family Law:
    Guidelines for Good Practice on Parental Contact in Cases where there is Domestic Violence
    (April 2002, available as archived material at **www.dca.gov.uk**)
Family Division: *President's Ancillary Relief Advisory Group: Best Practice Guide for Instruct-*
    ing a Single Joint Expert [2003] 1 FLR 573
Family Division: *President's Guidance to Judges on the Implementation of the UK–Pakistan*
    Judicial Protocol on Child Contact and Abduction (May 2004, available at **www.
    reunite.org**)

Law Commission (Cm 7182): *Cohabitation: The Financial Consequences of Relationship Breakdown* (July 2007, available at **www.official-documents.gov.uk**)

Articles

Robinson, Neil: 'Developing family mediation: innovative approaches to ADR' [2008] Fam Law 1048.
Loram, John: 'Solicitors in the mediation room' [2008] Fam Law 262.

Useful contacts and websites

Advice Now

www.advicenow.org.uk/living-together

ADR Group

Head Office

Grove House
Grove Road
Redland
Bristol BS6 6UN
DX: 99884 Redland Bristol
Tel: 0117 946 7180
Fax: 0117 946 7181

London Office

46 Essex Street
The Strand
London WC2R 3JF
Tel: 0207 632 7157
E-mail: info@adrgroup.co.uk
Website: www.adrgroup.co.uk

Association of Contentious Trusts and Probate Specialists (ACTAPS)

c/o Henry Frydenson, Chairman of ACTAPS
Frydenson & Co Solicitors
Central Court
25 Southampton Buildings
London WC2A 1AL
Tel: 0203 178 8777
Fax: 0203 137 8877
Email: henry@frydenson.co.uk/
yvonne@frydenson.co.uk
www.actaps.com

Association of Child Abuse Lawyers (ACAL)

Suite 13, Claremont House
22–24 Claremont Road
Surbiton KT6 4QU
DX 57714 Surbiton 1
Tel: 020 8390 4701
Email: info@childabuselawyers.com
www.childabuselawyers.com

Association of Lawyers for Children (ALC)

c/o The Administrator (Julia Higgins)
PO Box 283
East Molesey KT8 0WH.
Tel/Fax: 020 8224 7071
Email: admin@alc.org.uk
www.alc.org.uk

The Bar Pro Bono Unit

The National Pro Bono Centre
London WC2A 1JF
DX 188 London Chancery Lane
Tel: 020 7092 3960
Email: enquiries@barprobono.org.uk
www.barprobono.org.uk

Broken Rainbow

(Support and information for lesbians, gay men, bisexuals and transgender people experiencing domestic violence)
Tel: 08452 60 55 60 (admin, 10–5 pm)
0300 999 5428 (helpline, 9 am–1 pm, 2–5 pm)
Email: mail@broken-rainbow.org.uk/

info@lgbt-dv.org
www.lgbt-dv.org

Cafcass National Office

6th Floor
Sanctuary Buildings
Great Smith Street
London SW1P 3BT
Tel: 0844 353 3350
Fax: 0844 353 3351
Email: webenquiries@cafcass.gsi.gov.uk
www.cafcass.co.uk

Childline

Tel: 0800 1111

Child Maintenance Enforcement Commission

Existing Child Support Agency Cases: See Child Support Agency
New application queries: See Child Maintenance Options
www.childmaintenance.org

Child Maintenance Options

Tel: 0800 988 0988 (Mon–Fri 8 am–8 pm;
Sat 9 am–4 pm)
www.cmoptions.org.uk

Child Support Agency

PO Box 55
Brierley Hill
West Midlands DY5 1YL
Tel: 08457 133 133 (national helpline)
www.csa.gov.uk

Citizens' Advice

Myddleton House
115–123 Pentonville Road
London N1 9LZ
Tel: 020 7833 2181
www.citizensadvice.org.uk
www.adviceguide.org.uk

College of Mediators

3rd Floor
Alexander House
Telephone Avenue
Bristol BS1 4BS
Tel: 0845 65 85 258 (Mon–Fri 8.30 am–6 pm)
Email: admin@collegeofmediators.co.uk
www.collegeofmediators.co.uk

Community Legal Advice

Tel: 0845 345 4345 (Mon–Fri: 9 am–8 pm;
Sat: 9 am–12.30 pm)
www.communitylegaladvice.org.uk

Dyn Project

(Welsh helpline for male victims of domestic violence)
Tel: 0800 801 0321
Email: info@dynwales.org
www.dynproject.co.uk

Families Need Fathers

134 Curtain Road
London EC2A 3AR
Tel: 0300 0300 110 (office),
0300 0300 363 (helpline, 6–10 pm)
Fax: 020 7739 3410
Email: fnf@fnf.org.uk
www.fnf.org.uk

Family Mediators' Association (FMA)

Grove Road
Grove House
Redland
Bristol BS6 6UN
Tel: 0117 946 7062, 0808 200 0033 (helpline)
Fax: 0117 946 7181
www.thefma.co.uk

Forced Marriage Unit

Foreign and Commonwealth Office
Tel: 020 7008 0151
Email: fmu@fco.gov.uk
www.fco.gov.uk

Gingerbread

255 Kentish Town Road
London NW5 2LX
Tel: 020 7428 5400, 0808 802 0925 (helpline,
Mon–Fri 9 am–5 pm, Wed 9 am–8 pm)
Fax: 020 7482 4851
E-mail: info@gingerbread.org.uk
www.gingerbread.org.uk

Her Majesty's Courts Service (HMCS)

Complaint Handling and Enquiries Team
Zone C, 1st Floor,
102 Petty France,
London SW1H 9AJ
Tel: 0845 456 8770
Fax: 020 3334 4087
E-mail: customerservicecshq@
hmcourts-service.gsi.gov.uk
www.hmcourts-service.gov.uk

International Child Abduction and Contact Unit (ICACU)

The Official Solicitor
81 Chancery Lane
London WC2A 1DD
Tel: 020 7911 7127
Fax: 020 7911 7105
DX 0012 London/Chancery Lane
E-mail: enquiries@offsol.gsi.gov.uk
www.courtfunds.gov.uk/os/icacu.htm

The Law Society of England and Wales

General enquiries

113 Chancery Lane
London WC2A 1PL
Tel: 020 7242 1222
DX: 56 London/Chancery Lane
www.lawsociety.org.uk

Law Society Accreditation Schemes

(For Children Panel, Family Law Panel and Family Mediation Panel information packs)
113 Chancery Lane
London WC2A 1PL
Tel: 0870 606 2566

Law Society Practice Advice Service

(For matters of legal practice and procedure)
113 Chancery Lane
London WC2A 1PL
Tel: 0870 606 2522

Solicitors Regulation Authority

(For issues of professional conduct)
Solicitors Regulation Authority
Ipsley Court
Redditch
Worcs B98 0TD
Tel: 0870 606 2555 (*Professional Ethics helpline*)

Legal Services Commission (LSC)

4 Abbey Orchard Street
London SW1P 2BS
Tel: 020 7783 7000
CLS Direct tel: 0845 345 4345
DX: 328 London
www.legalservices.gov.uk
See also Community Legal Advice.

Ministry of Justice

102 Petty France
London SW1H 9AJ
Tel: 020 3334 3555
Fax: 020 3334 4455
DX 152380 Westminster 8
www.justice.gov.uk

National Association for Child Support Action

NACSA
PO Box 4454
Dudley
West Midlands DY1 9AN
Tel/Fax: 01384 572525
E-mail: enquiries@nacsa.co.uk (free general enquiry support)
admin@nacsa.co.uk (subscription enquiries)
www.nacsa.co.uk

National Association of Child Contact Centres (NACCC)

Minerva House
Spaniel Row
Nottingham NG1 6EP
Tel: 0845 4500 280/0115 948 4557
Fax: 0845 4500 420
Email: contact@naccc.org.uk
www.naccc.org.uk

National Association of Guardian ad Litems and Reporting Officers (NAGALRO)

PO Box 264
Esher
Surrey KT10 0WA
Tel: 01372 818504
Fax: 01372 818505
Email: nagalro@globalnet.co.uk
www.nagalro.com

National Family and Parenting Institute

430 Highgate Studios
53–79 Highgate Road
London NW5 1TL
Tel: 020 7424 3460
Fax: 020 7485 3590
Email: info@familyandparenting.org
www.familyandparenting.org/

National Family Mediation

Margaret Jackson Centre
4 Barnfield Hill
Exeter
Devon EX1 1SR
Tel: 0300 4000 636 (Mon–Fri: 9 am–5 pm)
Fax: 01392 271945
E-mail: general@nfm.org.uk
www.nfm.org.uk

Office of the Official Solicitor and Public Trustee

81 Chancery Lane
London WC2A 1DD
DX 0012 London/Chancery Lane
Tel: 020 7911 7127
Fax: 020 7911 7105

Email: enquiries@offsol.gsi.gov.uk
www.courtfunds.gov.uk

Relate

Premier House
Carolina Court
Lakeside
Doncaster DN4 5RA
Tel: 0300 100 1234, 0845 130 4010 (helpline, Mon–Fri 9.30 am–4 pm)
E-mail: enquiries @relate.org.uk
www.relate.org.uk

Resolution

PO Box 302
Orpington
Kent BR6 8QX
Tel: 01689 820272
Fax: 01689 896972
DX: 154460 Petts Wood 3
Email: info@resolution.org.uk
www.resolution.org.uk

Respect

1st Floor Downstream Building
1 London Bridge
London SE1 9BG
Tel: 020 7022 1801 (general enquiries), 0845 122 8609 (Respect phoneline, Mon–Fri 10 am–1 pm, 2–5 pm), 0808 801 0327 (men's advice line, Mon–Fri 10 am–1 pm, 2–5 pm)
Fax: 020 7022 1806
Email: info@respect.uk.net
www.respect.uk.net

Reunite

PO Box 7124
Leicester LE1 7XX
Tel: 0116 2555 345 (administration), 0116 2556 234 (advice line)
Fax: 0116 2556 370
Email: reunite@dircon.co.uk
www.reunite.org

Rights of Women

52–54 Featherstone Street
London EC1Y 8RT
Tel: 020 7251 6577 (advice line, Tues–Thurs
2–4 pm, Fri 12–2 pm), 020 7251 6575 (admin-
istration)
Fax: 020 7490 5377
E-mail: info@row.org.uk
www.rightsofwomen.org.uk

**Serious Organised Crime Agency
(SOCA)**

PO Box 8000
London SE11 5EN
Tel: 0370 496 7622 (24 hr)
www.soca.gov.uk

Southall Black Sisters

21 Avenue Road
Southall
Middlesex UB1 3BL
Tel: 020 8571 9595 (general enquiries),
020 8571 0800 (helpline, Mon–Fri 10 am–
12.30 pm, 1.30–5 pm)

Fax: 020 8574 6781
Email: info@southallblacksisters.co.uk
www.southallblacksisters.org.uk

**Women's Aid (freephone national
domestic violence helplines)**

England: 0808 2000 247 (24-hour, run in part-
nership between Women's Aid and Refuge;
Language Line and BT Type Talk available)
Wales: 0808 80 10 800 (8 am–2 pm, 8 pm–
2 am)
Scotland: 0800 027 1234 (24-hour)
N. Ireland: 0800 917 1414 (24-hour)

Women's Aid Federation of England

Head Office
PO Box 391
Bristol BS99 7WS
Tel: 0117 944 4411 (general enquiries)
Fax: 0117 924 1703
Email: info@womensaid.org.uk/
helpline@womensaid.org.uk
www.womensaid.org.uk

Index